Legacy of Faith

A Journey of Discovering God's Plan in My Life

DEE DOMINO

ISBN 978-1-0980-6453-2 (paperback)
ISBN 978-1-0980-6454-9 (digital)

Christian Faith Publishing, Inc.
832 Park Avenue
Meadville, PA 16335
www.christianfaithpublishing.com

Printed in the United States of America

Contents

Introduction: The Question of Faith 5

Part 1: Sundays..9
  Section 1. The Beginning 11
  Section 2. A New Life..17
  Section 3. Put On Your Church Clothes....................22
  Section 4. A Visitation of the Spirit 24

Part 2: The Journey Begins...29
  Section 5. School Days 31
  Section 6. Journey to Adulthood................................36
  Section 7. I Came to Believe.......................................39
  Section 8. Journey of Deception 43

Part 3: Transformation..49
  Section 9. Returning to Insanity 51
  Section 10. Journey to Believe 54
  Section 11. On Bended Knees 58
  Section 12. Journey of Transformation.......................62
    Point 1—God My Provider..............................66
    Point 2—Picking the Weeds in My Garden 67
    Point 3—Listening to the Spirit.....................69
  Section 13. A Call to Serve 72
  Section 14. A Journey of Lessons 80
    Lesson 1: Spiritual Blindness 80
    Lesson 2: Parent Rules.....................................81
    Lesson 3: God's Reality....................................83

Lesson 4: Youthful Experiences Can Shape
                Your Future 84

Lesson 5: Not for Sissies 87

Lesson 6: Seeking the Father's Face 88

Lesson 7: The Great Deceiver 89

Lesson 8: Believe What You Cannot See 90

Lesson 9: Every Knee Must Bow 91

Lesson 10: Transformation 92

Lesson 11: Serving Others Is the Highest Calling 96

Part 4: Summing It All Up 99

My Understanding of Faith 101

Our Story 105

Life in Ministry 108

Meet the Family 110

The Alexanders 112

The Gift of Motherhood 115

The Next Generations 119

The Seven Faith Keys 122

    Key 1—Ask Him 122

    Key 2—Consider Him 123

    Key 3—Confess to Him 123

    Key 4—Believe Him 124

    Key 6—Receive Him 125

    Key 7—Walk with Him 126

Acknowledgment 127

Introduction

The Question of Faith

Have you ever asked these types of questions? Does God really exist? How can I know if God is real? Is heaven or hell real? What happens when I die? Why should I pray to a God I cannot see? How can we know the Bible is reliable, historically or theologically true? These and many more questions are often pondered, yet where are the answers? How do we know that anything regarding faith is real?

It is perfectly normal to ask such questions. I believe most people want answers for how or why we exist. Do you believe what scientists say about the start of our existence? Or do you ascribe to what is known as biblical truths? There is an astronomical number of religious practices throughout the world, and as vast as the world is, in every culture, there are beliefs that shape the minds of its people. The practice of connecting to a higher power is quite common. Why is it that we are so driven to connect to a higher power? People all over the world practice some form of worship, even if it comes down to believing in oneself. Whatever we chose to believe, it seems we are all searching to find peace and acceptance. Whether it is a strut of a dance, playing an instrument, the chanting of words, the singing of hymns, or giving homage to a statue, these types of practices have played out throughout our history. I believe it is innate in all of us to wonder how we came to exist.

This world is full of life in every form, and as we look upon all living things that move upon the earth, there has to be a moment when we ask ourselves how this planet came to be. Nature speaks loudly to us that we are not the authors of its origin. Man did not put the sun in the sky to shine by day or the moon and the stars to light up the night. He did not fill the oceans with creatures beneath the sea or cause rivers to form. Man could not have shaped mountains and valleys, cause vegetation on the ground to grow, or cause the tallest of trees in the forest to appear. He did not create every species of birds to fly, and he did not cause the many creatures that crawl or walk upon the ground to be. It's reasonable to question how humanity and all of creation came into existence. These thoughts could only conclude that there has to be something or someone bigger than us that exists. I encourage all the seekers of this truth to ponder this for one moment. My hope is that you will use this as a starting place to say, maybe God really does exist. I truly believe the universe in all its glory awaits all of us seekers to look for and desire answers.

I too was once a skeptic and did not believe. I only believed in God because my parents said he exists. I thought if you cannot see it, maybe it does not exist. Oh, but life is the best teacher of God's truth. It has a way of waking you up. I came to the understanding that just because I do not believe a thing, that does not mean the thing does not exist. I know how difficult it is to see beyond all the smoke and mirrors. It's difficult to see the truth of God's existence, especially when we see hypocrisy. When we look at the flaws and fallacies in mankind, it only causes more doubt. We base unbelief on the failed examples around us. Yet we have only one example that God provided, who was the perfect representation of God himself, Jesus.

That's why I wanted to tell my story. I wanted to leave this book for others to know what happened in my life when I asked the question—does God really exist? We each will one day have to make a decision about what we believe about God. The question of faith will come up, and you will have to choose a side. Either you are a believer or you are not, there is no getting around it. Have you asked the question yet? If you have not, will you? What will be your story? And will you share it with others? I encourage you to ask friends and loved ones if they believe God exists, and if so, why or why not? As I share my story, my hope is that you will ask yourself what you believe about God.

My parent's decision to impart faith in my life was truly a God idea. He orchestrated my faith's future by using my parents and so many others. I could have had any parents in the world who were atheists or some other religion other than the Christian faith, but I believe God gave me parents who would lay a foundation of knowing Jesus Christ. There is a verse of scripture that says, "Train up a child in the way that he should go, and when he is old, he will not depart from it" (Proverb 22:6). Well, that scripture became true in my life. My parents took that verse to heart and acted upon it. Now go with me to discover how I came to faith and what God taught me along my journey.

Part 1

Sundays

Section 1

The Beginning

My memory fades back to seven years old. I was the seventh born of nine children. We lived in the city of San Francisco, which was home to me up until the age of thirteen. My parents were people who were both born in the French Colonial State of Louisiana. I have no knowledge of either of their childhood experiences or what brought them together, but somehow, they found each other. They left Louisiana and came to California, seeking a better life. My mother had already given birth to three older siblings, and they each had different fathers from the last six of us. We didn't spend much time with two of my older brothers whom I only remember coming around every now and then. They were already grown by the time the rest of us were born. My oldest sister stayed with us, to help my mother care for us.

My parents had a restaurant for some time during our early years in the city, so my mother sold many of her fabulous dishes in the restaurant. I remember running around the restaurant and sitting at the tables during lunch, waiting for my mother's dish of the day. There was one time she cooked a pig pie. Now I know that doesn't sound so appetizing, but it was better tasting than you would think. She was known for her peach cobbler, pound cake, and sweet potato pies. She made creole dishes like jambalaya, étouffée, gumbo, and the best cioppino you would ever taste. The family was surely blessed to have a mom who knew her way around the kitchen.

The Golden Gate Park was in close proximity to the restaurant, so we often had picnics in the park. Thinking about those days brings back some of my fondest memories of family togetherness. My siblings and I spent many weekends exploring attractions along the beach area of San Francisco. We would spend hours in the haunted house, and nearby was the zoo, where we could see all the animals. There was an exhibit called the Laughing Lady. Her laughter was infectious, and we would stand there laughing with her until our guts were sore and tears ran down our faces. We would run in an out of these mirrors, which you could see your reflection multiplied and you had to figure out how to get out. My parents knew they could keep us entertained in these types of situations. We played hide-and-seek for hours, and when our parents got us home, we were exhausted.

My father and his brothers were quite the hunters and gatherers, So, the food was plentiful. I remember we always had a basement in many of the homes we lived in. I think it was to store all the meat they brought back after my father and his brothers returned from hunting weekends. We were not allowed to go in the basement, but I remember the smells and would see multiple spices of fresh deer, pigs, and pheasant. We had large freezers and extra refrigeration for storage. We never went without food. We laugh at the fact that our parents now live in the city, but they were still acting as they lived in the countryside of Louisiana. I could only imagine how they may have hunted and gathered food back there. We always had a backyard full of fruit trees and vegetable gardens. My mother was into canning, so we always had a pantry of goods. My mother planted collard greens, tomatoes, and cucumbers in addition to the hanging produce. We had lemons, plums, cherries, peaches, apples, figs from which she spent hours preserving these foods for our family. At times, I would help her prepare the canning items and make sure all the jars had the proper tops for closing. Cooking with my mom was her way of spending time with me. Outside of that time, she was often preoccupied with caring for our big family. I think that was the way she emotionally connected to me without saying how she felt about me.

I have fond memories of playing throughout the neighborhoods and having lots of friends. My father had other brothers living in the city. We spent many weekends with the aunts, uncles, and many cousins between the families. We consider each other not just family but friends and playmates. We never had to be alone or go without family being there for us. Spending time with family was valuable back then, and we appreciated the time we shared. The most memorable times with our family happened every Friday night when our parents would go to one of our uncle's houses to play cards. They enjoyed gathering to compete in bid whist. We always had food on the table, and occasionally they would take a sip of whiskey. No other time had I ever seen my father or mother drink. The children had their own activities of course. We tried not to disturb the adults as we teased one another, running around the backyard, waiting for the food to be served. We were very competitive in the game of jacks and checkers. Those were the good old days when we had no worries or concerns of any kind. In those days, we did not have cell phones or electronics of any kind, so we had to be creative in how we played and made things fun.

The next biggest day for our family was gathering on Sunday morning. We started the day before by laying out our clothes and getting our baths before the night ended. It was quite an ordeal to get us ready for Sunday service. My mother was good at planning our routine, so we would be dressed, fed, and ready to go on time. I remember us sitting on the floor or in each other's laps if we had to, but we managed to cram ourselves in the car, and off to church, we went.

My father was a deacon or a so-called preacher in the church. That's what we use to call men in the church who have not been ordained to preach but made sure they looked as important as the pastor. He didn't legally have the title, but I believe he felt called to preach. My father got us to memorize the books of the Bible by promising us money whenever we could recite each book perfectly. This took some time, and we became competitive in the process, but this was a way to get us interested in the process of learning the Bible. I did not realize it back then that the legacy of my dad's faith was being passed down to our generation. The influence of faith was being produced not just through our parents, but through aunts, uncles, and our cousins. Everyone played a role in shaping our beliefs about God. Sometimes the church consisted of just family members, but we kept God in the center of any gathering we had. In the African American culture, God was preached, and the Bible was the foundation of our lives since slavery. Because of the history of being beaten down and rejected by society, God was their only hope. Our ancestors know how important it was to pass the faith on to the next generations.

My mother kept a sharp eye out on us while my dad was sitting in the deacon area of the church. If anyone of the elders or ushers caught us acting up and my parents were told, we knew there would be a severe punishment that followed. We sat on that role, lined up like bowling pins, acting as if we were interested in what the pastor was saying. It was more like entertainment for us. We would look forward to seeing the sisters who would shout and fall out onto the floor while the usher waves the fan over their faces. If the message got good to the pastor, we saw a spittle shoot out of his mouth as he preached. They would hoop and holla and jump around the pulpit. After service, some people would ask, "So what did you get out of that message?" And the response was usually, "I don't know, but he surely did preach." Church was very predictable we watched the theatrics, but miss the truth of the message.

Singing in the choir and competing with other choirs was another tradition that was very common. We would visit other churches after morning services ended, so sometimes we didn't get home till ten o'clock at night. All of us had to sing in the choir whether you could sing well or not. We spent so much time at church; you could say, It became our second home. We did not complain to our parents, but I thought we believe this is what all families did. We had no idea other people did not necessarily believed in God or spent time in church as we did. We had no exposure to other cultures, just ours.

When I turned seven years old, my parents decided the six of us were ready for baptism. We were all put in white robes, and we lined up one by one to be dunked in the baptismal pool. I professed my faith in God at the age of seven, but I didn't understand what that meant or the symbolic reasons why people took this step. We did it because that's what the church required, and our parents said it was time to do it. I stepped into the pool of water, but for what? Because my parents told me to do it, so I went down a dry sinner and came up a wet sinner. At my age I couldn't make an intelligent decision in this matter. No one took the time to explain that the act of baptism, was identifying with Christ's death, burial and resurrection. The pastor spoke a few words over me and told me to cross my arms. He leaned me back, and in I went. One by one, we all when down and back up. We scrabble back to change out of the drenched garments and return to play as usual.

After the first service, some of the women of the church would prepare these fabulous fried chicken dinners while the pastor was bringing his message to a close. It was hard to focus on church as children because the smell of fried chicken and biscuits made it difficult to sit still. This was quite normal for our congregation as we disassembled and headed to the social hall of the church. We gathered for prayer again before we consume that fried chicken dinner. The children would run around playing during the cleanup, and before we knew it, the second service was underway. We would laugh and eat candy as we sat in the pews, hoping not to get caught by our parents.

Some Sundays, we would alternate locations to meet up. My mother had a reputation for being an excellent cook, so people never stopped dropping over for a bite to eat on Sunday. I love seeing all the great dishes of food as each family arrived. Dishes were laid out on the tables or in the areas around the dining room. You could smell the different aromatic flavors coming together like a well-played symphony. There were some awesome cooks in our family, so we never worried that we would not like the dishes being served. Sunday was my favorite day of the week all because of Sunday dinner. This was a tradition that was quite common among many African American homes, and the spirit of Sunday dinner will always be remembered.

By the age of seven, my birth father left after a bitter divorce with my mother. My sister told stories about my mother and the battles she fought with my father. After my parents were divorced and my stepfather came in the picture, he too was a man of faith, so our Sunday morning routine just continued. The details of the transitions of our lives were difficult to piece together. I only remember a short glimpse of my birth father being around. He was obviously present in the home for at least the first seven years of my childhood. Then the picture picked up with us visiting my dad at his new house. I remember running just around the corner, not far from where we lived to visit my father. His departure was one in which was not so devastating because he lived in close proximity. I felt he was still a part of our lives, and my mother was pretty understanding and tolerated us spending time with him. After our parents divorced, things change a bit. My dad's family was quite large and created a great space for us for family gatherings. My stepfather only had one brother living in the area, so having large gatherings ended, and we had to adjust how we spent time with our cousins, aunts, and uncles. Unfortunately, because of sickness, we lost some aunts and uncles, some moved to other cities, and one uncle committed suicide. We loss a number of family throughout the entire group of brothers. In spite of all the loses, we persevered and our family still kept the tradition of Sunday dinner alive.

It seemed as though my stepfather had been there all the time. My father faded out the picture of our lives as my childhood continued in the same fashion as before. As usual, our home was open for Sunday dinner and we continued inviting members from the church to join us. The only change on Sunday's was my stepfather's brother was now our new pastor. The traditions of the Baptist churches were the same, no matter which one you attended.

Looking back to the proverbs passage which told me to raise my children in the admonition of the Lord, I understood that passage and made the conscious decision that I would do the same with my children. I made plans for a peaceful and prosperous life, but even with that kind of hope, I had no crystal ball that could have predicted the future. Life took me through many phases and places, which brought me to where I am today. The seeds of faith planted by my parents took a lot of watering, but God made sure he was tilling the soil and fertilizing the soil of my heart to reap a harvest of fruit in my life.

Section 2

———————— ❦ ✦ ❦ ————————

A New Life

Leaving the city was painful to my thirteen-year-old mind, but change is inevitable. I just had to suck it up and move on especially since I had no say so in the matter. I missed my cousins, aunts, and uncles. My brother became ill with an asthmatic condition, which our parents were told. We needed to leave the cooler climate and go to a warmer location. So, my parents moved us about thirty-five miles from the city to a location nearby the hospital that was treating my brother. We moved into a new home, and I was not in love with the idea of going to a new school and having to meet new friends. The neighborhood was much smaller than living in the city. Everything was flat, no more hills to go up and down on our bikes and no more skateboards. We had to find new ways of entertaining ourselves. The whole idea sucked in my option, but we forged ahead into our new environment. The home was nice but a bit smaller than what we were accustomed to.

My parents probably felt since we were all a bit older now, it was time to downside. We didn't have a basement or two stories as all the other homes. This meant tighter quarters for us. We only had three bedrooms, so the bunk beds fit right into the space quite neatly, but space to play and find solitude, fell short of my expectations. I couldn't escape or hide the way I could in the past, so there I was, sitting in my room, hoping none of my siblings will come bursting in. I could hear my brothers and sisters running in the backyard, screaming, and playing with the baby chicks that hatched two weeks ago. The usual banging of the pots in the kitchen told me Mother was preparing a delicious dinner. I sat hoping it's one of my favorites, anything smothered in gravy with a side of rice. The smells that invaded the house brought joy to all of us. Whether it was my mother's cornbread, biscuits, or any one of her fabulous pies, we always knew whatever she cooked was going to be good. Dinnertime was the second-best time of my day, but right now, I was taking in the silence like a cool beverage on a hot summer day.

I loved reading books and getting lost in the stories or finding new adventures in the characters. It was a way to escape my boring life and live through the stories of one of my favorite books. Those moments filled my day with such joy. I kept my books hidden so no one would touch them. My drawings and my books were my only way to flee my boring existence and I treasured every moment. The peace was sweet, all mine, and I ran to it every chance I could get. Strangely, even when the room was empty, I never felt I was totally by myself. There was a warmth that surrounded me, and it was as if it was saying, "You're not alone." Its peaceful presence engulfed me, and it gave me a feeling of safety. The silence in the room was like the whispers of angels calling me to a place of calm. I was comforted there and became obsessed with getting back to it. Outside of that space of aloneness, I did not feel accepted. I had no insight about my mental state and why I felt better by myself. I just knew I was connected to aloneness. I liked being with me and only me. Some people struggle with being with themselves but not me. I fought for it. Sometimes one of my siblings would pop their head in the door to see if I wanted to come out and join them. I would say no, I'm fine, and quickly returned to whatever I was doing.

My dad was the only one who got it. He knew I was busy drawing or doing something that fulfilled me. He became my biggest supporter and was never disturbed by my disappearance. He knew I was safe, and I think that's all that mattered to him. On the other hand, there was my mother. She would rant on and on about me staying in the room. She was quite annoyed by my choice to isolate. It became a battle of the wills between us. She would make snipe comments when I did come out of my room, and there were times she would say, "Go back to your room since you haven't been out here all day." She didn't know I would be happy that she just gave me permission to go back to my quiet abode. I only came out to show my face from time to time to keep the peace, but I really hoped she would forget I was in my room. There were times she would insist on calling me out to watch TV or interact with my brothers and sisters. Sometimes she would ask me to help cook dinner to interrupt my activity. Little did she know, I found joy in cooking because it too was an expression of creativity. I resented my mother's medaling but realized she was not going to change her mind about me. That room was my salvation, and that spot on the bottom bunk bed was the only place I could call my own.

I watched as my sisters and brothers scramble round getting dress to go outside, as I sat quietly awaiting their departure. The still presence met me with open arms. I would often lose track of time, but I knew it was getting closer to the evening when I heard pots being wrestled from the cabinets. My mother would start to prepare dinner, and the noise went on for a few hours. She would shout out, "You all go wash your hands." The running of feet on the hardwood floors told me my time alone was coming to an end.

Our family was very routine, and when dinner was ready, the family always came to the table. Eating alone was not allowed in our home. Prayer was a requirement before every meal. We would hold hands, bow our heads, and thank God before we devoured our food. It didn't matter if we were at our house, or in the homes of my aunts and uncles, food was not served until we prayed. In most African American households, this was quite the norm back then, and still today, this continues to be a part of our cultural norm. As we sat down to eat, I would quickly shove down my food and disappear, unless it was my turn to do the dishes. Right after I finished, while everyone else took a seat to watched TV, I ran back to the room to finish a book or a drawing I started earlier. As an artist, it was easy to get lost in a drawing which sometimes took hours to perfect. In my world, it was full of color and words, and I was the boss of it. No one could tell me what or how to produce the masterpiece I was working on. My drawings got better and better although I had no formal training; I just had a natural ability to draw anything I saw.

Later in high school, I was able to take an art class with a teacher by the name of Art. I only got better, and I realize my ability was a gift from God. I never got tired of creating new images and would lose track of time, but my mother would snap me back to reality. I often look back and wonder if I had gone to school to enhance the God-given talent, what could I have become? Still today, I love to paint and draw, but it's more of a hobby now.

I was one of nine siblings. With six siblings still in the home at age seven, finding a space to be alone was challenging to say the least. I was immature back then. I use silence like a weapon and was determined not to be broken. I know now my mother never understood who I was and why I was hell-bent on not letting her change me. I later realized my mother did not see me as an individual with different gifts and desires, very different from my brothers and sisters. She did not know parents should encourage their children's differences. She wanted me to just fall in line and act normal like the rest of her children. I later had to forgive her for not knowing how to manage this challenge. I always say a book should have followed each child at birth. I realize now parents do the best they can with what they know. If you did not get treated right by your parent, then more than not, you will parent the same way you were parented.

My eldest sister shared a story and told me how harsh my grandmother was with my mom. My mother was doing what was done to her. This explained my mother's inability to be nurturing toward us. This was a cycle that I too did not see in the early years of raising my children. It may have come late for me, but as I became aware of this dysfunction, I was determined to break this curse in my life before I leave this earth. I began telling my children I love them, and I began to show more interest in their lives, as well as encourage the gifts in each of them.

My siblings too, never understood who I was. They teased me a lot. They picked on me because I was the darkest and the thinnest. They called me darky and shadow. I would cry and wonder why they were so mean to me. This behavior also reinforced my desire to isolate, and I tried to stay away from them as much as possible. In those days the topic of *bullying* was not spoken of as it is today. You just sucked it up and kept going. People believed that If the negative words did not kill you, they somehow made you stronger. Being bullied by family was more common than on the street. My third elder brother thought it was his job to ruff us up, cause fights between us younger siblings. We had backyard fights all the time. Two of my brothers loved to put on boxing gloves and go at each other. One day, I don't know how I got suckered into putting on the gloves, and before I know it, I was going toe to toe with my older brother. He hit me so hard I really did see stars. I was so dizzy I fell down and had to sit until my vision became clear again. Needless to say, I never let my brother put boxing gloves on me again. The fighting didn't end, and my older brother continued to push fights between me and a brother two years older than me. It did put a resilience in me that I was unaware of. I like how God can use all of your pain to prepare you for a future call. You will understand why I said this as my story continues to unfold.

Section 3

Put On Your Church Clothes

As I mentioned, my parents were people of faith, so church for us was mandatory. We attended church at least twice a week. Parents in those days did not ask you, "Would you like to go to church this Sunday?" On the contrary, you did as you were told, no question asked. You didn't talk back, stomp off, or give your parents a look that showed defiance, unless you were ready to pick yourself up off the floor. We were taught to respect our elders, and they did not have to live in your house. The neighbors, people at church, or just any adult stranger on the street, you gave honor to those who were older than you, especially people at church. The pastor, ushers, deacons, mothers of the church, you could be chastised by any adult around. If our parents hear we talked back to an adult, we could get scolded by that elder, then spanked, and punished once you got home.

Preparation for Sunday started on Saturday, and my mother was obsessed with every detail of getting our clothes, hair, and baths done the day before church. As a seamstress, she would spend hours sewing and making sure we were dressed in the best she could afford to provide. She rarely shopped for our clothes. Goodwill was also a place from which she frequently shopped. She was a good provider, homemaker, and we never went without food or clothing. The least favorite moment of my day would begin when it was time for us girls to get our hair pressed. This was part of the big production of making our appearance in church on Sunday morning. I would sit anxiously waiting for my turn. My mother usually left me for last because I had the longest and the thickest hair. By the time she got to me, she was tired and had no patience. I hated this weekly ritual and would have given anything to avoid it. You would think she should have started with me first to get it out of the way. I would tense up the moment I sat down. I could smell the hair that was burned earlier by the straightening comb, which was placed on the iron stovetop. I knew what was coming, and I could never feel quite ready no matter how many times we had done the routine. My hair would raise up on the back of my neck, trying to brace myself for if and when she would burn my ear, back of my neck, or forehead. I knew she was tired by the expression on her face. She pulled and comb my hair in such a way I could feel her frustration and disdain for the task ahead. This was not my happy place for sure. Next, we would have us pick an outfit that she had to approve of. Bath time was difficult because there was only one bathroom in the house. Each of us was given a number and a time to be out for the next child to get cleaned up before bedtime.

Sunday mornings, it was game on. My parents would wake us up, and we scrambled around like rats. We would race to get into the bathroom to brush our teeth and wash our faces. We took our baths the night before because trying to get six kids in the tub on a Sunday morning would be impossible. There was no such thing as getting up when we want to. We got up and did not leave our rooms without making our beds and cleaning up anything left out of place in our rooms. After we were dressed, we would race to be the first in line, to get a spot in the car. If you were last you got put in the most uncomfortable spaces in the car. You did not want to be the last one to be by the front door. They expected us to be ready to walk out to the car, and we did not dare linger. In those days, parents didn't call you over and over. You knew what the consequence would be if you made them late for service. We piled in the car, and off we went.

Section 4

A Visitation of the Spirit

My parents made the decision to move to a new neighborhood about thirty miles south of the San Francisco area. I noticed they didn't seem as interested in Sunday mornings as they once were. Finding another church was difficult since the neighborhood was smaller. We went to a Methodist church near our house, but I could tell my parents were not happy with the style of service. This congregation sung hymns, not gospel music. It was not upbeat, and you did not see anyone shouting, dancing, or swaying to the music. Everyone was stiff and we did not hear the usual amen response. We were raised in the Baptist church, so anything else was outside our comfort zone. Sometimes we would travel back to San Francisco and attend my uncle's church. The drive back and forth was now taking a toll on my now aging parents, so it became easier for them to read their Bibles at home. As we got older, I could see my parents pulling away from forcing us to attend church on Sunday morning. It seemed we now had to find our own way, but we never asked our parents why they stop going to church as they did before. They would still attend periodically, but they no longer pushed us to tag along. I later realized we were like sheep left in the pasture in need of a shepherd.

My younger sister who was thirteen years old at the time asked me if I want to go to a church called the Church of God and Christ. She was attending regularly and would come home excited about her experience. She would give me a vibrant description of the worship experience there. She talked about the testimony time and people dancing, shouting praise to God and being filled with the Holy Ghost as she called it. I had no clue what she was talking about.

"The Holy Ghost?" I asked, "What is that?" She had no explanation because just like me, we did not use the term in all our church experiences. I was curious, but I agreed that one day, I would visit with her, just not that day. She asked over and over for me to come, too, but I kept my distance. Something about it made me uncomfortable. When I stood outside the church, the music would get my attention, and it was almost like the music was an invitation to come in. But I was afraid to go in, so I waited for the doors to open to see my sister run out to meet me just to hear the story she would tell me that day. My sister was different. She was always pretty humble and a nice person. She was not as rowdy as some of my other siblings. I think that is why her and I got along so well. I found myself acting as her protector when my brother picked on her. She was the youngest, the baby in the family. I felt she was special in a way, yet she too often times felt invisible in the wake of all the other bigger personalities in our family.

I remember my mother disciplining her and whipped her for doing something which I cannot even remember the reason, but I do remember my sister's reaction, which was not one of tears. She only said, "Thank you, Jesus." I thought this was quite odd. Here she is being stuck by the belt, and her response was, "Thank you, Jesus." I remember thinking she's crazy. Why was she thanking Jesus while she was being beaten by my mom? I never asked her why she said that, but it did make me even more curious about that church. She came out of the room and wiped away her tears, lay on her bed, and we never talked about it. I thought to myself that she has been going to that church for months, what were they doing to her? She was praying a lot, reading her Bible, and we didn't talk as much as we used to. I became so curious that on the next Sunday, I got dressed and followed her there.

As we walked in, I remember feeling like I did in our old church. The women were dressed in their Sunday best; they had their hats on. And as the pianist cranked up the organ, you could feel something was coming. People started to praise God, and one by one, people came up to testify of God's goodness in their life. Now for anyone who have not experienced a service where people testify, trust me, if you ever had to attend this type of service, make sure you eat before you go because you will be there for a while. These people went on forever, and all I kept thinking was how long was this going to take, being that the pastor had not even begun to preach. I sat wide-eyed and paralyzed waiting to see what would happen next.

The pastor finally got his turn to preach, and by this time, the church erupted in people shouting, praise dancing, and the pastor asked if anyone wanted to be prayed for. My sister immediately leaped from her seat and went to the front. I stayed seated, watching as the festivities continued. Suddenly a woman in front of me fell back, and the people around her caught her, and as she when down, she was jerking around on the floor. The emotions in the room went so high as people were singing, clapping their hands, shouting praises to God. I remember feeling that angelic presence I used to feel in my room. I felt lifted if I could describe it that way. I didn't have a care in the world. I saw my sister running around the church, praising God. That has never happened in all the years we went to church. I thought, *What is this?* I knew something happened to my sister that day. I didn't know what, but she was changed. She was quiet, always thanking God for the good and the bad.

A few months later, my sister became ill and was taken to the hospital. She was diagnosed with lupus, and we all were surprised by this news. We never heard of any such disease, so our family spends days and weeks running back and forth to the hospital. I remember seeing the nurses and doctors coming in the room; it was like a revolving door. They took blood samples after blood samples, hoping to find a way to save her. They frantically searched for a cure, but my sister's life was slowly slipping away. I remember thinking, *God, why her? She was the good child, the one who was the least problematic of all the kids.* Yet her life ended, and the family was in shock as we grappled with the news of her death. We never understood how this could have happened so suddenly, but I knew deep inside of me I was chosen to see the day of my sister's spiritual awakening. I believe it was God's plan for me to be at that church to witness my sister's spiritual rebirth. He wanted me to know there was something beyond merely going to church. I witness the visitation of his divine spirit. My sister left this earth extremely happy, and when I saw her in the hospital, it was as if she knew she was never coming home again. As the years past, the memory of my sister's conversions faded away, and I became less interested in going to church.

Part 2

The Journey Begins

Section 5

School Days

Years after the death of my sister, I became curious about a boy in my neighborhood. I was smitten by him and started sneaking around to see him. We hung out and played around as many kids do, but after he kissed me, I started to have feelings for him. Every chance I could, I would run down the street to play with him. I had to hide this from my parents of course because they would never approve of me seeing a boy at thirteen. He started to make sexual advances toward me and I knew I was not ready. He became frustrated that I was not ready for sex, so he found another girl who would do what he wanted. Our friendship ended as a result of this, so, we stopped seeing each other. As I went through puberty, I had many crushes along the way, but I was determined to keep my virginity. I like boys, but not like that. I had heard of girls getting pregnant, and I was determined that I was not going down that road.

High school opened up many new and exciting adventures for me. I was a good student who excelled in my studies, sports, dance, art, and cooking. I played on the baseball, basketball team, and ran track during the year. I was one of the top badminton players in addition to participating in the synchronized swim team. Besides art, I loved the competition, so playing any sport was pure joy. My life really changed when the state decided to bus children because of desegregation laws. I do not know how they chose students from among the schools, but my name was put in the hat. My parents were told that I was included in the group of students who were to be sent to a school outside of our neighborhood. I was pissed that I was abruptly taken during my second year of high school. I felt the world being snatched from under me. I had worked so hard to be the best in my class and on the field of sports. I had proven myself to be one of the best in all I did, and now I had to go to a place where no one even knew my name, except for the people who were bused along with me. Talk about culture shock; we all were in for a bumpy ride.

The school's population was predominantly White, and it became very apparent that our presence in the school was not welcomed. I will never forget how long that ride felt that day as we anticipated the reception of our arrival. As the bus entered that school, someone approached the door and asked the driver not to let anyone off the bus until notified. We were unaware of the challenges we would have to face once we stepped off that bus. We sat on the bus for what seems to be hours. Students were looking at us from every direction. It felt strange to be looked at like we were aliens from another planet. Their reactions were one of bigotry and hatred simply because we were African Americans. Up to this point in my life, I don't remember experiencing racism. I was aware blacks had died in slavery, and some black leaders were killed, but this was up close and personal. I never felt so unwelcome in all my life. Once the word came down that we could get off the bus, we headed to the cafeteria to where the principal spoke to us and briefed us on what would be our first day on campus. After receiving our schedules, we each had to leave and walk into those rooms where you knew you were not welcome. It was one of the hardest things I faced in my teenage life, but once again, here was another hurdle to climb and another lesson to learn. I walked into my class while all eyes were fixed on me, and as I entered the classroom, little did I know, they too received a pep talk from the teachers about the new changes. It was strange being the minority and not the majority as it had been in my previous schools. My former school was predominantly black with a few Whites and Hispanics. I'm sure they must have felt the same way I was now feeling.

I was very athletic prior to coming to this school, so I decided to use my athletic ability to fit in and feel a part of the new environment. I ran track, played basketball, tennis, and was a good swimmer. I was able to find commonality in the love of sports, and this broke across the lines of color. In sports, as my fellow players saw how good I was, the doors of acceptance began to open, and new friendships were forged. Later I found myself conflicted with wanting to fit into my new environment and keeping relationships with those from my neighborhood. I still rode on the bus with these people, so I had to walk a fine line not to appear I had betrayed my unspoken allegiance to them. This balancing act was difficult; I began distancing myself from the students from my neighborhood. This could leave me alone in case of discord. I needed to know if it came down to a fight, my people had my back. I didn't trust this new crew like I trusted the old crew. We all said if anything jumped off, we were going down together.

I was changed by this experience, but I never realized the psychological effect it had on me at the time. My life took a turn at this point, and new challenges started to arise. I got involved with a group of kids. I knew them from the neighborhood but had never associated with them up to this point. Now faced with a different environment and a different crowd, I felt a need to fit in, so I started cutting classes and hanging out with a group of students. We had spots on campus that we would congregate, and sometimes we would sneak off-campus. The more I got involved with them, my boundaries became weaker. I use to laugh at them when they were high, but my curiosity started to open me up to the possibility of wanting to experiment. I went from sipping out of their bottles of beer to taking puffs off their cigarettes. Next thing I knew, I was popping reds, which was popular at the time. My grades were suffering, and I pulled out of my sports activities. The year was hard, and I later begged my parents to let me return to my former school. They agreed after watching my grades go down, but I hid the fact that I experimented using drugs and drinking and lost my virginity in the same year. Let me tell you it was not worth it. I allowed myself to believe this boy from the neighborhood really cared for me, and when it was over, I felt cheap and used. He and I never spoke or had anything else to do with each other after that day. In my ignorance, I had opened two dangerous doors that of addiction and sexual impurity. These behaviors were the gateway to the next chapter of my life.

The following year, I returned to my former high school to finish my last year of school. I got back on track, and my grades improved. I was able to catch up to graduate on schedule. I stopped the negative behaviors I picked up the year before. Things felt as though they were back to normal, but I was still quite shy, and I kept a selective group of friends around me at all time, people whom I trusted and those on a more positive path. The drinking and drug thing became a thing of the past, and I refocused my attention on academics and sports. I was back in an environment that empowered me to feel comfortable in my skin. It was that sense of belongingness and acceptance pulled me away from a self-destructive mindset.

I decided in my last year of high school to get a job. I found a job flipping burgers. The pay was not that great, but it was my first job, and I was excited to earn my own money. I was aware that earning my own money opened up new possibilities. The possibility of my independence was in reach, and I was focused on the prize of having my own space. I wanted to escape my parent's rules and restrictions. I think every teenager believes that leaving home is the ultimate answer when you are sick of following your parent's rules. Little did I know, footing the bill for freedom is costly. I had no clue where I was headed, and as soon as I graduated that night, I never returned home. I moved to my sister's apartment, the same night after crossing the stage and received my graduation certificate. My parents didn't attend my graduation because of the relationship between my mother and me was almost nonexistent. My step dad didn't want to rock the boat, so whatever she wanted, it's what he did. I was not as upset with him as I was with my mom because I know her influence had everything to do with him deciding not to come to my graduation. I didn't care at this point. I just wanted to be out of their house.

Well, freedom came, and I was now on my own. I got to decide how, when, and where I would go. I also had to foot the bill. It's funny how you don't seem to see all the things parents do for you until you get into the game of life where you are the responsible party. There truly is a cost for being the boss.

After High School photo

Section 6

Journey to Adulthood

After living with my sister for a few months, I realized I made enough money to get my own apartment in the same complex. My sister and I became neighbors until she moved away. Now I grew up—or so I thought—but I was unaware that making my own decisions also meant I had no one else to blame if things did not work out. I had to figure it out. My parents were not around to keep me from the impulsive self-destructive behaviors, or the mismanagement of my finances. There was no way I wanted to give them the satisfaction of seeing me fail. Parents did not talk about stuff back in my day; they just hoped it all worked out for us. It seemed it was taboo to be open and discuss the facts of life. I was too ashamed to let them know if things were bad. I did not want to hear I made a mistake leaving at seventeen years of age. I was determined to make it on my own. Going to my parents for advice would have been difficult. I was not open to hearing their feedback anyway. That would be like surrendering to the enemy. At least at the time, that's how I felt.

Leaving home at seventeen was impulsive, and I did not have a plan. I just knew I wanted to be on my own and very determined to survive. I was working and living alone. Later I had my girlfriend moved in, and things changed. Now I had a partner to hang out with and go clubbing with. We met a couple of guys at my job, who were friends, and we all started hanging out. God seem to move further and further off my radar. Sunday morning no longer was a day of worship but instead a day to recuperate from the night before. The new found freedom I had was a license to sin. To do what I want and when I want. Nobody could tell me when to come or go. The rebel was now on the move. No parents to make me get up, put on clothes, and drive me to a church to pray to a God, their God. I stopped attending church after leaving my parent's house. Now I was free to get buck wild as they say.

My friend and I were two young, inexperienced ladies, who later got involved with two guys older than us. We didn't realize what bad influences they were for us. We were drinking, smoking weed, doing other drugs, and having premarital sex. At the age of eighteen, I found myself pregnant with my first child with a man whom I was friends with, but not in love with. I later realized it was not in the best interest of myself or the other person to continue acting as if we cared about each other. We never discussed being in any permanent relationship, so marriage was never in the cards for us. I was now a single mother raising my son alone. I tried to keep my son's father involved in my son's life, but my efforts were not enough. My decision to bring my son into the world was my decision, and I took on all the responsibility that came with being a parent.

Once again, I was determined to handle it. Little did I realize the impact it would later have on my son and the consequence my son would suffer from not having a father in the home. I later realized I could not be the mom and the dad he needed. I found men in the big brother's club, hoping they would have a positive influence in my son's life. I worked hard to be a parent to my son and provide for the two of us. Yet being eighteen, I did not want to miss out on the days of my youth. I worked all week and looked forward to the weekend. I knew I could take my son to his grandparents. Even though his father was not actively spending time with my son, his grandmother especially adored my son. He was the apple of her eye, and she accepted him being there anytime I wanted to drop him off. Sadly, I used her love for him as my way to be free from all responsibility on the weekend. Her generosity and love opened a door for my sinful lifestyle, and I used that door as often as I could.

Now you might ask, where was God in all this? He was always there nudging me, telling me I was going in the wrong direction. Due to the lifestyle I was choosing, I was not inclined to listen. I ignored the voice of my spirit because it would mean turning away from the very thing I was running toward. I put God and the church on the "back burner." That's an old saying, you younger folks, might not have heard. There is another old saying which says, "We can get use to almost anything." I felt I needed to escape my responsibilities, even if it's just for a weekend and go clubbing as much as I could. This became a routine, but little did I know I was selling my soul to the devil. I called myself a "weekend warrior," which meant I worked all week but turned up on the weekend.

For the sake of not embarrassing myself or my children, I am not writing a tell-all book, so many details will not be in this story. Just trust me when I say, God was not pleased with what I did. Just know, I was headed in the direction of hell and not heaven. I almost wanted him to turn his head and not look upon my shameful behavior, but God sees all, so that was an impossibility. God's mercy was truly in my life. I could have been in car accidents, arrested, and jailed for breaking the laws of driving under the influence. I realized I could have taken the life of another or lost my mind as well. Thank God for his grace and care over me in the moments when I made some of the worst decisions of my life. Who knew becoming an adult could be so difficult and many times painful. Looking back, I can say I was clueless and wish I had more guidance through the process of growing up. "Oh yeah", I left the process when I left my parent's house, my bad.

Section 7

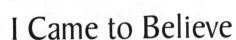

I Came to Believe

There was an incident that caused me to evaluate how my life was going, and it was the beginning of what I would call an awakening of my faith. I was certainly a believer of God, but my true quest and search to understand who he was came on the heels of a traumatic situation. There was a man in my complex whom I cross paths with periodically while getting my mail or leaving the complex I lived in. I would cordially exchange conversation from time to time, but little did I realize he had other plans. I was so naive and too trusting. I didn't have a car at the time, so if I needed to go shopping, I relied on others to take me to the store if I needed to purchase a large number of items. The neighbor made me think I could trust him. It was one of those moments that I needed help getting to the store to buy food for my son, so I turned to this guy for a ride. He quickly offered to accommodate my request and asked me to knock on his apartment door when I was ready to leave. I did not think of it as strange or felt uncomfortable with what he was asking, so I got my purse and hurry back down to his apartment. Upon arriving at his door, I knocked, and he asked me to step in for a moment while he grabbed his keys. I didn't think there was any reason why I should not go in, so I complied. Once I entered his place, I stood with my son in my arms, waiting while he went into his bedroom. When he came out of the room, he began telling me he was turned on by me, and I was going to turn him off. He quickly walked over to the door and locked it. I suddenly had a sinking feeling in the pit of my stomach and knew this could go very wrong. I was clenching my son in my arms, and I thought, why was he talking like this and he knows my son is present. I didn't know what to do at that moment. I felt if I tried to run out the door, it could make him react in violence. He turned then went into his room after picking up a knife on the table. I wanted to run and scream for help, but I was paralyzed with fear. In that moment, I knew this situation was beyond my control, and I needed an intervention. I remembered a verse of scripture that said, "If I call upon the name of the Lord, I would be saved."

I had no clue what that verse meant, but at that moment, I was in need of a miracle. I was willing to try anything, so I prayed a quiet prayer that went something like this, "God, if you are the one whom I have believed in all my life and you are the God whom my mother taught me about, you said whosoever called upon the name of the Lord shall be saved, please save me." The next thing I knew, this guy came out of the room, and I never will forget the look on his face as he removed the lock and opened the door. It was as though he was under a hypnotic spell, and he never spoke another word. I felt God was telling me I was free to go, so I ran out of there as fast as I could, and when I got back to my place, I fell to my knees in tears. The realization was so clear to me; God heard me. It was though he was standing in the room and took control of the situation, as soon as I called on him. I told God on that day, I wanted to know him better. The fact that I got out unharmed was nothing short of a miracle. I went back to my apartment and made sure my son was safe and fed. Later, I fell on my knees and cried, asking God to help me understand, and know the truth about his existence and power. I was so naive. I knew nothing about attempted rape or sexual assault. People in those days did not openly talk about those things as they do today. I never reported what happened to the police. The man never spoke to me or looked in my direction again. When he would see me, it was as if we had never met. I felt God continued to protect me from him, and I had nothing to fear.

I began fasting and praying and decided to go to church with a gentleman I was dating, who was much more active in the church than I was. We dated for a couple of years. He left for the military, and shortly after I decided, it was time to press into God. I attended church a few weeks later, continued to pray and search for a greater understanding of God. One night at church, I had an out-of-body experience. As I sat there, I could sense a presence around me. The preacher was calling for people to come forward for prayer and those who wanted to give their life to the Lord. I wanted to go up, but I felt an energy force holding me down. It was as though I was being stopped from lifting my body from the chair in which I sat. Perplexed, I looked around. Something was keeping me from moving, but what happened next was amazing. I felt a touch on my shoulder, and a voice whispered, "You can go now." I turned around in shock to see who was talking to me and who touched me, but I did not see anyone. The oppressive force I felt earlier was suddenly lifted, and I was able to move. I got up and went to the front so the preacher could pray for me. I stood there speechless because I had never encountered something of this magnitude in all my life.

As the pastor was talking, I remember seeing his lips were moving, but my hearing was on mute. I could see people in the church moving around me, but I couldn't hear a thing. I felt like I was in the twilight zone. I understood no one else knew what was happening to me. I could not fully comprehend what just occurred. When I felt that touch on my shoulder, a power surge penetrated my entire body. That power was not that of human nature but a spiritual one. The only way I could describe it is by saying it felt like pure love. I knew God had touched me; there was no doubt in my mind. This was the second time God was revealing himself to me. But why? I had an encounter with a power greater than anything I ever knew or experienced. I don't remember what the pastor said or who I encountered after that. When I left the church, I kept looking at the ground because I saw my feet walking, but I could not feel the ground. It was as though I was walking on a cloud. In addition, I felt as though I was encased in a protective bubble. I felt as if anyone were to shoot a bullet at me, it would have just fallen to the ground. I could not tell anyone. They would think I was making it up, or I had lost my mind. I really became more curious about God and wanted to get closer to him. What was he trying to convey to me? I realized I was chosen by God to know him in a way as the scripture says, "In the power of his resurrection."

My faith was deepened as I continued fasting, praying, and I spent countless hours reading the Bible. I wanted to know the God I met that night. I wanted to understand why God had chosen to rescue me from that horrible situation with the man in my apartment building.

Section 8

Journey of Deception

Some months passed, and I was now on a deeper spiritual path, but what I didn't understand is that there was another force at work in my life as well. The other dark force at work in my life was a deceiver of truth who operates through lies. The enemy of your soul is often cunning and will use whomever or whatever he can to take your focus off God. He or she can be extremely charming and brings gifts and opportunities at just the right moment. But little do you know, you become like Adam and Eve in that garden all over again. I let my guard down just long enough for Satan to send his servant to knock me off course.

There was a man living on the other side of the complex where I lived. We ran into one another quite often downstairs, near the mailbox area. He seemed friendly and had a sense of humor. We would exchange words, and I would walk away remembering his pleasant smile. He would tell his corny jokes and tell me how pretty he thought I was. Shortly thereafter, I found myself looking forward to seeing him and hearing his compliments. He was very sociable and not hard to look at. He drove an old Chevy, and the engine was loud, so it was easy to know when he arrived home every day. He knew where my apartment was, but I only knew he lived on the backside of the apartment building. As we continued to talk, he revealed he had a girlfriend, who was pregnant at the time. It didn't matter. I thought we were just friends. The friendship grew, and I could feel we had chemistry. He was a hard worker with a decent-paying job. In those days, if a man worked and could pay his bills, that was big. Now I did not intend to get involved, but because I was single and lonely, it was easy to fall for the thought he cared for me. I never understood why he chose to get involved with me.

He was a mechanic and very knowledgeable about cars. How convenient, right? Well, I did not own a car, so he was the perfect person to talk to about getting a car. He was all too willing to help me find a car, and I was able to get my very first car for one hundred dollars. I will never forget how happy I was. I could now drive where I need to go without having to depend on other people, and I found that very daunting. I could now take my son to daycare, go to the grocery store, or just hang out at the mall. It was a whole new level of independence. I was finally able to feel that I had accomplished another goal since leaving my parents and moving out on my own. This is where I say not everything that looks good to you, is not good for you. It was as if the devil sent his best agent, and I fell for it all.

About six or seven months into our friendship, he dropped over to my place with a bottle of wine, and he pulled out a joint. Well, you can only imagine how that night ended. Let's just say my walk on cloud nine with God took a nosedive into the pit of hell. My feet hit the ground, and I was no longer feeling all spiritual. I thought I had met the love of my life, the man of my dreams. Nope, it turned out to be the devil's advocate. He was deceptive, cunning, and I was blinded by my own lust. He was different from the other men I had met. I was vulnerable, barely nineteen years old, and immature. He was older and more experienced with women. I fell for his lines and his charm.

I had no clue what to look for in a partner, neither had I ask myself what I wanted in a relationship. This person did not know me, and I did not know a thing about him, yet there I was. A bottle of wine and a joint later, I went on an eight-year ride to hell. I thought I was in love, and that he loved me too. I failed to realize that if he was cheating on his partner with me, he was capable of cheating on me too. The Bible says, "Do not be deceived, God is not mocked;

for whatsoever a man sows, that he will reap." Talk about karma. What you put out into the universe can certainly come back to you.

I continued seeing him despite his disloyalty to the other woman, and I later found out he was doing the same with me. We both were being played. I was inflicting pain on someone else all the while having the insane thought that she was a fool. I used my youth to manipulate my way into his heart, trying to be his number one woman. I was clueless to the truth about my situation and of what he was up to when I was not looking. Now don't get me wrong. There were many moments of excitement throughout the first four years. I saw this through the lens of good sex, money he provided to buy what I needed, and a good laugh when things were good between us. I thought he was the one. I thought we would stay together forever. A year and a half later, I found myself pregnant, hoping we could make it all work. I stayed and tried to fight to be with the man who was now the father of my child. About the fourth year in, I found out he had four other daughters living in another state. I thought, *How the hell did that happen?* I guess each time he visited his home-town, he produced another child. This pattern continued, and yet he was obsessed with making sure no other man came remotely close to me. He continued to cheat on me while requiring my faithfulness to him. A friend tipped me off that I was being watched and followed whenever I left home. I couldn't believe this was true until he started to reveal he saw me in different locations far from where I lived. He would show up whenever male friends stop by and once chased a friend of mine in his car through the neighborhood. Another time, he showed up at my apartment with a gun and threatened my neigh-bor, saying he never wanted to see him at my place again. He also threatened to harm me if I let another man into my apartment all while he was being unfaithful to his girlfriend with me and unfaith-ful to me with someone else. Over the next two years, things only got worst. He became more possessive and obsessed with making sure no other man was stepping in on his territory. He tried to own me as if I was his toy. I thought it was flattering at first, but it was not so flattering each time I thought about the probability of him hurting me or someone else.

The straw that broke the camel's back for me is when he showed up at my house because he thought a man was in my home. He was right. Someone was there visiting, but it was not someone I was dating. I never knew how he knew that another man was at my place. It was like he had some weird radar. He quickly pulled into my driveway, and I told my guest to go out the back and hop the fence. Well, you don't ask why when you see a crazy person heading your way, so I instructed him to jump the fence and stay at my brother's place who lived next door. He was the brother of my sister-in-law. My partner was beating on the door, insisting to get inside, so when I knew the guest was over the fence, I opened the door and stepped outside and shut the door behind me. He wanted to come in to inspect my house, but I stood my ground that day. Why? I don't know. I think I had finally reached a breaking point and didn't care about the consequence of his wrath. I was threatened and taken by gunpoint, bare feet, and no jacket. He said he would kill me and leave me for dead if I left him. Well, I replied it would be better to die than spend another day in a relationship with you. He quickly backhanded me in the face for getting smart, as he put it. He drove me to a nearby duck pond and insisted I get out of the car. He ran around to jerk me from the car, but I only moved to the driver's side and would not let him take me from the car. This cat-and-mouse game continued for a few minutes, and suddenly he came to his senses. I don't know what shifted in his brain, but all I knew was he agreed to take me home and let me go.

That day was the first time I got angry enough to stand up to him, not back down, and he realized I meant what I said. I had said it before, but this time, I was not changing my mind. I was done with all the intimidation, stalking, threats, and control. I was his possession, and love had nothing to do with it. My eyes were finally open, and there was no going back. I was just a number among all the other women in his life. Although I was scared to leave, I knew I had too. I was so broken and tired by the time it ended, having severe migraine headaches. They were so severe that at times, I stayed in bed all day. I went to a doctor, and he asked a few questions, then commented as he looked at me. He said, "If you get rid of your headache, you will get rid of your headaches." I remember leaving that office with his words ringing in my ear. I knew what I had to do. God gave me the courage to walk away. All the baggage of our relationship started to be refreshed in my mind, and I no longer pushed my pain under the rug.

The worst memory of the early years of our relationship came over me like a wave in the ocean. During the early part of our relationship, his brother raped me, and the two of them went on as though it had never occurred. I was so ashamed and embarrassed; I never spoke of it or told anyone about it. He left me their alone with his brother after the three of us were drinking. He abruptly said he had to go make a run and left. His brother violated me, and I often wonder if it was planned by the two of them. It was dismissed as though it never happened, and I expected him to be outraged about it, yet nothing was ever said or done about it. I blame myself for being in their home that night. I won't go into all the details of that night, but let's just say, getting out of that sick relationship was the best thing I could do for myself. My daughter's birth was the best thing that came out of us being together, and as painful as it was, I kept my daughter in close relationship to her father. I began to focus all my attention on caring for my two young children. The stress and the pressure at times were quite overwhelming, but I was not going to let anything stop me from providing and caring for my children.

Part 3

Transformation

Section 9

Returning to Insanity

After walking away from the last abuser, I foolishly fell into the arms of a new one. My sister-in-law's brother started coming around, and I enjoyed his company. We could laugh and talk for hours. He was the fun guy whom you just love to be around. I had no intention to entering another relationship, but hanging out, drinking, and laughing with this now new guy led me back into a vulnerable situation. Little did I know I was walking back into some of the same insane stuff, just a different face. The insanity started once again, and this time with a full-blown alcoholic. You would think I would have connected the dots about alcohol being a common denominator, but I didn't. I had no understanding of substance abuse and how it reduced inhibitions, and my thought processes blurred, which weakened decision-making. I was a lot more vulnerable when I drank. The only difference was this was consensual, and I willingly became involved.

I lost another four years of my life getting involved with this dysfunctional and damaged person. Our relationship was volatile, and I never knew if he was going to hurt me or if I would have to hurt him. When he was sober, we laughed and enjoyed each other. The minute he started drinking, everything changed. He was verbally abusive, which later turned physical. I had gotten to the point that I could no longer tolerate his drinking. There was an incident that really convinced me once again that I needed to flee the relationship.

One evening, after he returned home from after drinking with a friend. It was apparent; he was intoxicated as he came in, talking loudly and slurring his words. I was talking with his sister, and as he began directing his comments to me, I knew things could shift to aggression. This become a pattern when he got drunk. He became mean, antagonistic, which many times left me feeling uncertain and on edge. I never knew if I need to protect myself, which is classic when you live with an alcoholic and abuser. I had hidden weapons in various places throughout the house.

As I stood with my back to him, he decided out of the blue to kick me. Now you got to picture me having a great time, laughing with his sister, and in the next moment, the atmosphere turns to a toxic environment of uncertainty. I had never been so humiliated in all my life. I had put up with a lot from him, but in that moment, something broke inside of me. It brought back memories of the previous abuse, and it was as if I went into a dark place. It was, as they said, the straw that broke the camel's back. Without saying a word, I walked into my children's room, where I had put a two-by-four piece of wood in the window. I grabbed it a quickly, went back into the room where he stood, and without thinking it through, I commenced to swinging, hitting him anywhere I could. I continued to beat him as he crawled toward the open door, trying to escape the whipping I was putting on him. I kept striking him with that wood with all my might. He ran out of the door, and with a final blow to his back, the wood broke as he fell onto the concrete porch. I ran back into the house and grabbed the biggest knife I could find. I came back outside and charged after him, and I imagined he saw the crazed look in my eye, the knife, so he started running. I was in hot pursuit, running down the middle of the street. The only thing that saved him that night was the fact he was a faster runner. My adrenaline was off the chart, and I, in that moment, understood what people meant when they say I snapped.

When I came to my senses and realized what I was about to do, I was scared. I stopped my chase, ran back into my house, locking the door behind me. After I got into my house, I thought, What if he comes back? What would he try to do to me? Or what could I do to him? I quickly jumped over my back fence, then over another neighbor's fence till I reached a friend's house, whom I trusted. I had so much energy in a single leap. I managed to jump three fences within seconds. As I beat on my friend's door, he opened and saw me with the knife, and with a calm voice, he assured me I was safe and could give him the knife. I was shaking in fear of what I could have done as my body started to subside. I could have landed in jail; my kids left without their mother. I imagined how this could have all ended, me stabbing him to death. It all became a big reality check. In that moment, I vowed never to date another man who would lay a hand on me or push me to the brink of insanity as I had gone that night.

The police came, and my sister-in-law told the police what happened, so they did not arrest me but took him instead. He had to get stitches in one hand, and he was told not to return to the home that night. The following morning, someone was knocking at my door. As I opened it, there stood another neighbor from around the corner. He asked me about the blood on the porch and on my door. I was embarrassed as I explained the previous night events. Later that afternoon, I had to face my boyfriend when he returned to the house. He tried to apologize, and I wasn't hearing it. I asked him to get his belongings and leave. I said it's over. I wanted nothing to do with him. It was impossible to avoid him completely because he was my sister-in-law's bother, and they lived next door. My now ex continued to drink and get high whenever possible, so life for him just continued to be a downward spiral. I later found out he was seeing another woman behind my back, so I was glad it had ended. He later died in his forties from liver disease as the result of his drinking.

Here was another example of the unmanageability in my life. These bad relationships, as painful as they were, acted as a conduit in my journey toward God. God use them and many other situations to develop my faith. As I look back, I had to thank God for his mercy over my life. I could have been badly hurt or even died at the hands of the people whom I thought cared about me.

Section 10

Journey to Believe

My reckless behavior led me to repeated heartache again and again. It was like jumping from a plane without a parachute. My man picker was certainly broken. I began to ask myself some serious questions. Why do I keep running into the same kind of men? What is wrong with me? Why can't I find someone who will love me and treat me right? I started to believe I had an invisible sign on my forehead that told men it was okay to use and abuse me. God inspired me to dream bigger and started to show me that I had the power to make decisions that could affect positive change. I realized the thing that held me back most was me. I could choose to love myself. I didn't need another person to validate me, and the only one who could make my life better was me. I felt God was trying to protect me, but I needed to stand up and be protective of myself. I had to stop giving myself to men who did not have my best interest at heart, men who didn't deserve me. I was a good woman, and I had to see myself as the prize. I had to set new boundaries for myself and others. I began to lift my standards and aim higher. I vowed to myself to stay out of relationships until God brought the man in my life who would love me the way God does. God helped me to see I was living below what he called me too be. Being single became a blessing and not a curse. I could not make up for the lost years, but I had choices, and I could choose different.

I had moments of clarity and glimpses of what my life could look like if I had made different choices, seeing a vision of myself as happy and prosperous. God kept trying to get my attention, but I was so busy trying to enjoy my youth and survive that I took my eyes off God. I allowed myself to be enticed by the desires and urges of my flesh.

A side note here, in the teenage years, I was clueless to what it would take to have a meaningful relationship. Even beyond those teen years, most people don't understand what's required. Most of us just stumble our way into sex and then oftentimes marriage. Still clueless about what is required to have a loving relationship where two people seek to put the other above themselves. If I can give some word of wisdom to younger men and women, I would say one word—*wait*. Becoming an adult does not equip anyone with enough life experiences or wisdom to manage or handle the difficulties that relationships bring. My experience of betrayal, sexual assault, verbal and physical violence was no way to live. As they say, I was looking for love in all the wrong places. I lost all desire to seek out what I call love. I learned much more than saying a word; you must understand of the origin and the true meaning of that word. It wasn't until I defined love from the context of the biblical understanding of the Bible. I had no idea what to look for in my relationships. I believe God gave me this revelation, which caused me to push the pause button. I was void of a plan and needed to rethink what was important to me and what it meant to truly love another human being.

The Bible is very clear and gave me a wonderful collection of stories that depicted the same struggles I encountered. All I had to do is turn to the Word of God, and the answers I needed were right there. I did not understand that spiritual laws exist, just as natural laws do. The choices I made had a ripple effect and came back to me. Have you ever done something you knew was wrong and thought it was behind you, and later the very thing you thought you got away from came back to revisit you? It happened to me over and over. The mistakes I was making may not have been visible to anyone else, but it was becoming very visible to me. I heard the small whispers of God's gentle voice telling me I was headed in the wrong direction. I used to ignore that voice inside, but I later learned that I better pay attention. I came to understand those whispers were there for a reason, and that I should pause and pay attention. The bull in a China shop approach to life was foolish. I learned how to stop, pray, and listen to the wisdom of the Holy Spirit. I saw my life unraveling, and I needed an intervention to bring my life back to sanity. God's love gently guided me back to the faith I grew up with. Today I understand I am nothing without God, and he is the most important focus in my life.

I was unaware of AA's twelve-step program when I was abusing my body with drugs or alcohol. In the program of AA, clients are given twelve steps, which guides them in the process of recovery. In step 1, which says, "We admit we were powerless over alcohol/drugs, that our lives had become unmanageable." When I evaluated my life, that's exactly what state I was in. I was a functioning user. Another term people used back then, I was "a weekend warrior," which describes a pattern of partying hard on the weekend then returning back to my responsibilities during the week. I soon saw drugs and drinking was interfering with the relationship I had with my kids. A wake-up call for me was watching a friend lose her home, car, and eventually her child. I praise God for giving me the clarity to see where I could end up and the wisdom to see I was powerless over drugs and alcohol. I watched her life go down, and I fell to my knees and asked God not to let me end up like her.

By the grace of God, I was able to avoid that path of jail, and the next time I saw her was in my classroom of the local jail. She was surprised, as well as I. She looked at me and asked how I did it. I simply said God. She acknowledged she could see the difference between our decision and said she wished she would have allowed God to come into her life. I said it's not too late. We never saw each other again after that day. I think it was too painful for her to return to my class. This was the person who introduced me to the drug that could have destroyed my life. Only by the grace of God, I turned away cocaine, which took its toll on many lives in the eighties.

Other members of my family were involved with drugs, which made quitting more difficult because it was readily available. Instead of them being role models, they presented more opportunities for me to use. The dysfunction of drugs and alcohol is that you don't care who you take down with you. I didn't know at the time that I was genetically predisposed to addiction. My family tree was full of drinkers and drug users. My older brothers were using, and I lost a younger sister after she became addicted to drugs. She was heartbroken after losing her daughter in a fire. This event sent her into a deep depression, and I believe she just stopped caring. Her husband blamed her for not saving their daughter that night, and the marriage ended in divorce. She was never the same after the death of her daughter, and she spiraled out of control. She moved to Los Angles, running from the problem, owing a dealer money. She changed locations, but unfortunately, the change of location did not change who she had become. Once again, she started taking drugs from a dealer, whom she owed money, and sadly when he caught up with her, he took her life. She suffered and did not deserve to leave this world in the way that she did. She was only in her mid-thirties. She left behind a son, who also suffered the loss of his mother.

This was another wake-up call for me. I certainly did not want that to be the story of my life. The thirst was growing inside of me, and I knew I needed help. The insanity was real. I would get high and pray for God not to let me die. God saved me over and over from my stupidity. I can't tell you how many times I drove under the influence of a substance and yet live to talk about it. That was pure grace. I know that the angels of God very much kept me safe when I knew I could have ended up crashed on the side of the road. I praised God each time I think about how I could have died but lived instead. As I saw the powerlessness of addiction creeping up on me, I also sensed God's Spirit calling me. It was undeniable that I needed help to break the circle of darkness that surrounded my life. This brought me to step 2, "We came to believe that a power greater than ourselves could restore us to sanity." God was my only hope. I need restoration and knew in my heart that God was my only way out. I was too ashamed to tell anyone what I was going through and how my soul was crying out for change.

Section 11

On Bended Knees

I was broken and ready to take the third step. "I made a decision to turn my will and my life over to the care of God as I understood him." I started to think the God I understood would not have chosen me to be in these situations. I believed he loved me more than I was capable of loving myself. His love was calling me to change my life, and I finally wanted to listen. I cried after that day and asked God to transform me. I wanted him to strip me of the pain and misery I had chosen. I was the perpetrator of my own pain, and I could not attribute my suffering to anyone else. My brain was hijacked, and I listened to its call for more drugs. The addictive brain will tell you, "You need more." I thought if only I could buy a larger quantity, I could have it all to myself. Now this would probably have killed me or sent me to the nearest emergency room, but that's how the addiction speaks to you. In my mind, I could only think about the feeling, not the consequence of my actions. Short-term gain, not the long-term pain.

My income tax was coming, and I was determined to use it for the very purpose of copping more drugs. I began to isolate, pushed away friends and family, unless they too were trying to get high. I could feel my character changing, and deep inside of me, I understood how wrong this was. The weekend warrior stuff I could sense was wrong on every level. Yet I would lie to myself and justify being a hardworking single parent who just needed to unwind. After all, I had to reward myself in some way, or so I thought, but God had another plan. My sister-in-law came by and said she wanted to go to church. I told her I too had been thinking about going to church. One week before I got that income tax check, we went to church. Boy, did God show up for me big time? As the preacher called for those who was in need of rededication to come, I quickly leaped from my seat and ran toward the front of the church. As the choir sung, tears flowed down my cheeks. I felt as though I had return home, just like the prodigal son. When I left the church that afternoon, I felt good. I felt I had finally taken a step in the right direction. My sister-in-law and I went two separate directions that day. She returned to the old life of drinking and drugs, and I walk into a new life with Christ.

Now I don't want to make it sound like I just drove off into the sunset, and everything in life was blissfully wonderful. My first challenge happened as soon as I got back in my car. The temptation to smoke a cigarette was waiting for me. I had left a pack of cigarettes on my dashboard before going into the church. I had been smoking for ten years at this point. I came face-to-face with one of my biggest addictions and had to immediately decide. Here was my first test of faith. I could either believe that God was able to give me the power I needed to stop smoking or operate out of pure willpower. I said a quick prayer and tossed my cigarettes out the window. My desire in that moment was to turn my will over to God's care.

Now you might ask, "Did the cravings go away that day?" I would say no. However, walking by faith is just that. You may not see the results of the decision in the moment, but if you hang in there, the fruit of the choice will come. The testing of my faith didn't end there. I came home, and I vowed to allow God to transform me into the image of his son. I now, by faith, had to take step 4, which is, "Made a fearless and morale inventory of ourselves." I had to look in the mirror of my life and see the ruins of my mental, physical, and emotional pain. My life was in need of serious repair. I reflect back on all the wasted years of wrong choices and the pain I put myself through. I was aware of the kind of pain that could be passed onto my children if I remained in the same state. It was difficult to look in the mirror and be truthful about the inventory taken of my life, and what it really said about me. It started with recognizing I was living in sin, and that the sins in my life was controlling my behavior. I needed God to empower me to do what I couldn't do alone.

Two weeks after my return to church, I asked to be rebaptized to symbolize my rebirth. I read about Jesus being baptized by John the Baptist, so I decided to be baptized once again to symbolize my recommitment to Christ. It was my hope to resurrect from the water into the newness of life just as Christ did when he died on the cross and rose from the dead. I thought if Jesus went to the grave for my sins, then I too needed to respond to God's command to be baptized. I can truly say God worked a miracle in me that day. On that day, I lost all cravings for nicotine, and I never had a thought or desire to smoke again. That was God's power working in me, no doubt. I did not do this on my own. I never touched a cigarette again. It's been thirty-four years to date since that time. Praise God!

Well, the devil is always busy as we often say. Just because I had decided to turn my life over to God, it didn't mean the world around me was changing. The weekend ritual of hanging out with friends or family was still in effect. Friday night came around, and as usual, I was invited to indulge in alcohol, cigarettes, and drugs. I had to make a decision over and over each time the opportunity presented itself. I was either going to allow my flesh to rule or my spirit. I remember going into the room of a family members house, and they were doing what they always do, and I was offered something. The enemy of my soul was in full effect, and he would use anyone or anything to take me out. The urge to partake suddenly was like a knee-jerk reaction, and without question, I took one hit of the substance. I did not even so much as ask myself the question what, why, or even if I should do this. After I had inhaled, I heard a voice in my soul say, "I have already delivered you." I immediately turned, put down the pipe, and ran out and left the house. The Spirit of God had spoken to me, and I now was convinced the word of God was alive and lived inside of me. I fell on my knees, and I thank God for delivering me. I had to believe it to receive it. Believing that the words of the Bible will come to pass is not always easy, but I had to put my faith into action. I believe it was the ingredient that set me free, his power mixed with my faith enabled me to break free from the chains of all addictive substances.

This experience once again proved to me that God was there. He was listening to my cries for help, and he was willing to give me the power to overcome. I realized I could bring all my problems to him, and he would assist me in the answers. In every situation, I could go to my father in heaven, and he would help me work it out. It became critical to keep faith at the forefront of my life. Life without God for me is like trying to cross a large river in a small boat without a ruder or a paddle. I never want to just drift in life, hoping I will somehow make it to the other side. I had to make God the ruder, the paddle, and the captain of my ship. To God be the glory. Before you get to excited, it was long from over. One thing you got to understand when Jesus comes into your life, he does great things in you, but it's a process. Transformation takes time, and what I know today is as long as I live in this body, the nature of sin is still alive in me. Christ in me is the hope of glory. God sent his Spirit to dwell in me, and as I continue to depend on his power, my desire to sin is less and less. It's not over. Let's continue with my story and I will explain how this process of change unfolds.

Section 12

Journey of Transformation

Trusting God is an act of blind faith. I was not sure if the steps I made would lead me to my desired outcome, but that is why it's called faith. It truly is about what the scripture says, "Now faith is, the substance of things hoped for, the evidence of things not seen." When you ask God for answers, most often you will not get an answer at that moment. Believe me, when I tell you, he hears your prayers, but he often waits to see if you will believe he can give you what you ask. God tells us to ask whatever we desire, but if we lack the faith to believe he can deliver what we ask, it hinders our results. When I asked him to change my life, I didn't know how, but I believed he could. I did not know what surrendering my life to God would mean, but I did think as messed up as it was, anything else had to be better. I continued to shift my perspectives. I had two children depending on me to be a better parent and not just hear me talk about God. I could not tell them it was not God's will for any of us to live a sinful lifestyle, especially since I was still living in sin myself. Well, change was more challenging than I had imagined at the time. I struggled with wanting to have what I deemed as fun and living out the truths in the Bible. The battle between the spirit and my fleshly desires became very real.

As I read the Bible, the revelation of God's truths became clearer. I was in a fight for my eternal soul. The scripture says, "For we do not wrestle against flesh and blood, but against principalities, against powers, against the rulers of the darkness of this world, against wickedness in high places" (Ephesians 6:12 KJV). I felt this darkness and knew that the truth of that scripture was right. I learned I had to fight if I was going to endure, so I found in the book of 2 Corinthians, which says, "The weapons of our warfare are not carnal, but mighty through God to the pulling down of strong holds." When you are bound by any kind of addiction, whether it is food, drugs, alcohol, sex, crime, or any other habitual practice that has a stronghold in your life, God is the remedy. Take my word, the forces of darkness will be working to keep you imprisoned in whatever trap you find yourself in.

The scripture became my food and my drink. The Bible says man or women shall not live by bread alone. That simply means we are not fed spiritually by the food that we eat or the water we drink. It takes spiritual nutrients, and it's not found in your local supermarket. It is found in the life-giving power of the word of God. Many people fail to believe the truths written in the Bible. They will say things like, "Oh, it's just a book written by man, or it's just about history." But for us who have encountered the life-changing power of Jesus Christ, we can testify of the realness of God's word and his spirit. If you ask most Christians why they believe in Jesus Christ and the Bible, they will share not only what they've read in scripture, but the life-changing experiences they've walked through as a result of encountering God's truths.

Our God is relational, and he is as real to us as any human relationship can be. I can tell countless stories of God's divine nature working in and behind the scene of my life. The scripture also told me if any man or woman be in Christ, they are a new creation, and old things are pasted away, and behold, all things are new. Well, I can tell you I needed the new one because the old one sucked. I was in relationships that did not honor God, and this had to change. I knew sex before marriage was not God's will for my life. I vowed to him to surrender my body, just like all the substances that had me bound. I needed to challenge the abuse, drug use, wicked thoughts, lying, stealing, and so much more. My work was truly an inside job. The road to holiness is long. God has to do surgery on the heart of a man or women. Giving up the outward sins is a lot easier to do, then transforming the evil intent of the heart. I have found even on my best day, I still struggle and find myself casting down evil thoughts or slip into gossip and slander, speaking harshly about a brother or sister or not treating a stranger right, not to mention not loving your neighbor as yourself. God said the greatest commandment is to love God with all your heart and love your neighbor as yourself. Well, that is easier said than done. It is a hard command to follow and that's why Christ died for me. In my humanity, I see my failure to keep the Bible's teachings on a consistent bases, so I praise God for his plan of salvation, not based on my works but on his grace alone.

I read a scripture where the apostle Paul was writing to the Roman church. He talks about believers being dead to sin and alive to God. He said, "What shall we say then? Are we to continue in sin so that grace may increase?" Then he answered the question, "May it never be! How shall we who died to sin still live in it? Or do you not know that all of us who have been baptized into Christ Jesus have been baptized into his death?"

"Hold the phone. What are you saying?" I asked myself. I have to put to death my lustful desires to have sex with men I was not married to? I read on. If you drop down to Romans 6:6–7, he says, "Knowing this, that our old self was crucified with him, in order that our body of sin might be done away with, so that we would no longer be slaves to sin; for he who has died, is freed us from sin."

Wow, I know this is a mouthful. Let me make it simple for you. When Christ died and he rose from the dead, he took upon himself our sins on the cross. When he died, he gave us the Holy Spirit, who assists us with the endless power of God to resist the temptation and the grip of sin. We have the ability to call upon the assistance of God's spirit. That, of course, is a choice that we must make whenever we are tempted. We no longer have to practice sin; we can choose to walk away. Resisting our desires and submitting them to the Spirit is our responsibility. He will never force his will on us. What we don't understand is that as long as we live in these earthly bodies, that choice will have to be made over and over again. You may wonder why do we still sin. That is the condition of the fallen state of man.

When Adam and Evan sinned, the curse of their sin was transferred to all of us. The result of one man's sin, we were all declared guilty of sin. Doesn't seem fair, but you will have to take that up with God himself. Yet the scriptures tell us the choice of another man, Christ, when he became the sacrifice and died on the cross, he became the ransom for all of us. Understand that God himself declared that all have sinned and require death as the payment of that sin. Yet in his love and mercy, he decided to send his son to pay the penalty that should have been handed down to all mankind. My eyes were open to the reason why I needed to receive Christ. I had acted on God's command which says, if I confess to the Lord Jesus and believed in my heart that God raised him from the dead, I will be saved. Christ paid a ransom for my life that I could not pay, and with that payment, I was given the gift of eternal life. I am eternally grateful for the blood that was shed for me and I started to work on surrendering to God every day.

In my transformation process, I had to become less dependent on my self-will and more dependent on God's power. I asked him to lead me and guide me through the process of change in every aspect of my life. The next challenge I faced was a decision to surrender my sexual life over to the care and will of the Father. At this point, I had not entertained marriage, but reading the scripture that said it is better to marry than burn in my lust. So, guess what I was now saying, "God, help me to not sin against you in this area." I chose to wait on God's provision for a marital relationship and return to a life of celibacy. I had to trust that God knew the desire of my heart and would provide the right person for me. That desire was to live a life pleasing to God and in obedience to his word. I chose God over a man. I understood that men came and went, but God said he would never leave me or forsake me unlike most of the relationships I had. I learned that I could choose to love myself first and not allow others, no matter who they were, to treat me disrespectfully. With this knowledge, I no longer was a victim and could live my life in victory, so I chose to wait. I want to share some key points I learned on the journey of change.

Point 1—God My Provider

I saw him provide for me when I had nothing. When money was scarce, I watched him send people into my life to open up avenues where provision came. I remember driving to church on my last tank of gas, and after sitting down, a woman sat next to me. Once the service ended, she slid over to me with her fist balled up and said, "God told me to give this to you." She put money in my hand. Now you might say that was a mere coincidence, but I know for a fact that no one but me and God knew my financial condition at the time. I was a hairdresser, and out of the blue, when money was short, people would knock on my door, asking if I could braid or cut their hair. When I couldn't feed my kids, things like this happened over and over. I was on welfare, and although I was getting assistance from the government, I didn't just rely on that but trusted that God would provide and direct me. He gave me the wisdom to use my resources in a way that provided beyond what I thought was possible.

I met a gentleman, who was a real estate broker, who talk to me about buying a house. I was able to save twelve hundred dollars, which provided me with the funds I needed as a down payment on my first home. I was twenty-one and not many twenty-one-year-old's buy houses, especially being on welfare. Another time God sent help was when my hot-water heater broke. I prayed and asked God for help, and you would not believe it; a neighbor showed up at the door, and as we talked, he told me he was trying to get rid of a water heater from his grandmother's garage. He ran back, picked it up, carried it on his back, and installed in my garage, free of charge. The next time I saw God's hand being inexperienced as a home-buyer, I overlooked paying my home taxes, the first year. Hello, God is a provider, so I prayed not just what to do but asked if he would work out how I would pay the debt. The bank called two weeks later and said they had taken care of the back taxes and informed me I would see a slight increase in my payment until it was paid in full. God was with me in everything. He put it in my heart to follow the advice of my mother who told my sister to buy a home, and she shunned that advice, but not me. I learned the importance of listening to others, getting wisdom from someone more experienced than me, and it played a big role in my learning process. I began to seek out older women in my life who could give me spiritual wisdom, and sometimes, they used their motherly advice as they looked out for me, just as they would for one of their own daughters.

God has promised to be with me in every situation and work things out for good. For me, they are not mere coincidences, but I watch for the hand of God to be in the midst of every situation, and yes, even the bad situations. In each of these scenarios, I did nothing to change or arrange the outcome. Prayer was my only response. I have so many stories I could tell like this one, and they continued to occur throughout the years till today. God has demonstrated his love and provision for my needs and in the lives of so many others around me. He is a God of promise, and he is a presence to walk us through every circumstance. He is there in the good times and in the most difficult of times.

Point 2—Picking the Weeds in My Garden

In prayer, God revealed many things I had ignored or hadn't thought about. He revealed the truth to me about my life, and I was able to see my fallen state. Sometimes it is hard for me to look in the mirror and see the person looking back at me. Here was another area of my life that required serious transformation. I needed a change in every area of my life, and oftentimes, it was too big to tackle. But now with God, all things became possible. Weeding out the bad was complicated. Abusers were so much a part of my world I couldn't always see them in the blindness of wanting to be loved or accepted. There were so many instances of abuse I almost become numb to it. I have brothers who were physically and emotionally abusive. Fighting them became my norm. I didn't expect the patterns of fighting to continue after years of sibling rivalry. I just wanted peace.

One day, I became angry with a so-called friend, whom I had this one-sided relationship with. I was doing all the giving. I would drive out of my way to pick her up whenever we spent time together. She yelled at me while driving in a parking lot, telling me I made a wrong turn. She started to belittle my driving because I missed a turn going out of a driveway. When I dropped her off that evening, I started to playback what just occurred. It was like someone hit me in the back of my head and said, "Wake up fool." She was complaining about my driving, but I thought, *she has a car. Why doesn't she ever pick you up and drive sometimes?* A light went on in my head. "Wait a minute, why is it that I drive everywhere we go? When was the last time she volunteered?" I asked myself. If she doesn't like my driving, she can go to…you know where I was going with that.

Another situation occurred with another friend whom I called to check up on regularly. I devoted myself to her needs and went out of my way to visit her. As I sat in her house, waiting for her to enter the room, I began to think about why she hasn't ever come to visit me. I realized I never required that she make the same effort because I was so accommodating. I began to go through all the people I was in relationships with. I fell on my knees and asked God for wisdom in this matter. I realized most of my relationships were very one-sided. I was a natural giver and had no boundaries. I didn't even know what the term *boundaries* meant. I had many takers, but I did not think I was important enough to ask or require others to give back. I learned that people really do treat you how you teach them to treat you. Whatever patterns you allow to form, people just continue with what you display as acceptable. Boy, was this a wake of call for me. I took the kick-me sign off my behind that day. God gave me a vision of a field that was dead. Everything had dried up and withered on the ground. He said, "You need to teal the soil of your garden, remove the weeds and thorns in your life." I took that vision and started to let go of people who did not produce good in my life, those who abused my friendship and took my kindness for weakness. I put them in the rearview mirror of my life, and as I move forward on a new path, I promised myself I would not Keep dead things in my garden ever again. This changed everything for me as positive results in friendships began to blossom and as I was becoming more aware and selective.

As a Christian, I thought you just had to turn the other cheek and be nice to folks even though they are not nice to you. I didn't need to go out of my way to be kicked. Being nice doesn't mean being a doormat. I learned loving God was first, but loving myself was necessary. Becoming a Christian did not mean I should not take care of my emotional and physical well-being. If you are like what I just described here, take an inventory and weed out those people who do bad things to you, who show no interest in your life. People don't always think of you the way you may think of them. They may have other ideas of what they want from the relationship. I have learned to evaluate the fruit. If they do not reciprocate the love you give to them, maybe they are not for you. We all want to be loved, and when we are exposed to rejection, it can be painful. Most people seek acceptance. I went to great lengths to find love, even if it was from all the wrong people. Some of those people were just as broken or needy as I was and had no capacity to give me what I needed to build me up.

Understanding the sinful nature of the human species was eye-opening. We don't realize there is nothing we face that the Bible doesn't give us an example of a scripture to reassure us that God understands our need. This is why people say the Bible is the (BIBLE) *b*asic *i*nstruction *b*efore *l*eaving *e*arth. Everything I go through, I can consult the Bible for wisdom and comfort. If you doubt what I am saying is true, just try it for yourself.

Point 3—Listening to the Spirit

My first encounter with the Holy Spirit was so powerful; I will never forget it. I was raised Baptist and was not taught anything about the Holy Spirit's power in my life. God sought me out and, as the Bible said, gave his precious Spirit as a guide. After coming back to the Lord and getting baptism for a second time, I became more sensitive to the spirit's leading. It's hard to share this area of my life with others because it's something you have to experience to know what I am saying. I was not only baptized by water, but I experienced the inward baptism of the spirit with the evidence of speaking in tongues as the Bible describes. Now I know this is somewhat controversial for some people, but it is my testimony and my story. I will take my experiences with God over what anyone else chooses to believe about God. Throughout the years of praying and a listening to the Holy Spirit has guided me to success in many areas of my life.

Learning to be still and listening to whispers of the Holy Spirit, he became a way to know what path to take. God's plan was different than the one I may have chosen, but he has certainly proven he is the best planner I can have. I never planned to write a story about my spiritual journey, but here I am telling my story, hello. Even today, I am asking for his guidance for the next steps. I depend on the Holy Spirit. Believe me, when I tell you, he is so personal that if I lose something, I will stop and ask the Holy Spirit to help me find it. Sounds crazy not to a believer who knows God's voice and experience his Spirit's leading.

I lost my remote control in the house, could not find it to save my life, but I stopped and prayed, "Holy Spirit, I need you to help me find the remote." Well, as I waited for his answer, I heard the Spirit said, "Look at the recycle trash." I was like, "No way! How did it get over there?" Well, without question, I went and looked in the trash and didn't see a thing. So, I said it was not there, and in that still small voice, I heard, "Dig deeper." I went back and took all the items out of the trash this time, and there was my remote at the bottom. Now I know how out of touch this may sound, but believe me when I tell you it is the truth.

That same voice kept me at a stoplight driving to work one morning. I did not step on the gas because I was praising God at the stoplight, and I felt the Holy Spirit's presence in the car. The light was green on my side and red on the other, and before I knew it, a car came through the light on my left at about eighty miles per hour. If I have not been communicating with God in praise, I would have been possibly killed. That driver never stopped and would have hit me if I had taken off at that moment. I was very aware that I was spared from a tragedy that day.

The Bible says we are to be led by the Holy Spirit. If you ever encountered the Holy Spirit of the living God, there is no questioning that God really does exist. The Bible tells us that Jesus, when he ascends back to heaven, he left us a comforter, the Holy Spirit who now leads us and guides us. God said the only way we know God is by the spirit of God. If these words are difficult to understand, then you have not experienced his present and power. Every believer who has come face-to-face with the power and present of God has a story of the power of the Holy Spirit. If that has not been the case in your life, I would say, "Fall on your knees and ask God to come into your heart, as you accept, Jesus Christ as Lord and Savior." I promise you if you seek God, you will find him. He is waiting. I did, and he showed up.

Section 13

A Call to Serve

The call to service began with me actively participating in a Bible study group with other church members. The groups were designed for each individual to build deeper relationships and get to know one another in a deeper way. We discussed the Bible and prayed for one another and all those who work in ministry. We shared laughter, great meals and sometimes very personal struggles. For example, one of our members became very ill and was diagnosed with cancer, which was life-threatening. When you hear the word *cancer*, most of us usually think the worst is to come. For our brother, this was the case. His wife was overwhelmed with grief for her husband, and she was a full-time mother of two children. The group members immediately stepped up to assist and care for this family. I had never been a part of something so powerfully significant as this demonstration of God's love begin to work through each person who participated in helping. I was very involved with spending time with my dying friend. I had not had this experience with any family members or anyone else I knew in my life. I knew God would want nothing less from me but to give comfort to him and assist the family. We took turns cooking, cleaning, and spending time with the children. This rotation of compassion went on until the husband passed, and we were all there to support the wife and children. Months later, our brother was put to rest, and we mourned with the family. I found such a sense of purpose in service, and I also felt I was fulfilling the command of God to love one another.

The next experience of services started when a friend talked to me about getting involved with the chaplaincy ministry of our church. I felt God pulling me in this direction, so I said okay, and he became my mentor and help me through the process of preparation to enter the jail system. Shortly after I got clearance to enter one of the nearby facilities, we started on a road I hadn't traveled before, but I knew me and my church brother was not alone. We had faith that God was with us. I could not imagine what the experience would be like or knew what to expect. I just knew in my spirit that God was saying go. The first time I entered the jail, I will never forget the sounds of the environment. In the parking lot, I was told not to bring any personal items in, except my ID.

As I entered from the outside, I had to stand in a waiting area until I was signed in, and my ID was taken until I returned to check out. We were then escorted into the inside of the jail and asked to wait in a room that was designated for the meeting room. I watched as officers moved inmates through corridors, and you could hear voices in every direction. Men who were sometime in handcuffs passed by, and they all were dressed in orange jumpsuits. I felt like I was under the watchful eyes of those in the environment, whether it was by the inmates or the officers. You certainly knew you were in their house, and your presence was under very close scrutiny. As we waited for the men to come in, we quickly prayed for God's mercy to fill our hearts and the hearts of the men. As the men started to come into the room, I remember feeling outnumbered since I was the only female present. I reminded myself through the evening that God had a purpose for me being there. I continued shadowing the man whom I looked up to as my mentor and continued to follow his lead for the next nine years. We traveled to all the local jails and sometimes to San Quintin prison for church services. We always went to the men's area of the jail or prison. I had to ask myself why. Oftentimes, I was the only women in the room. Now looking back, I can tell you it was because God had a plan, but it was not revealed until later in my journey. I was not afraid or felt intimidated by being the only woman in a sea of men. I just continued in my faithfulness to do the work of ministry. Only you can feel that kind of confidence when God has your back. All fear was gone, as I walked in God's authority and with the power of the Holy Spirit.

Years later, I left that church, and this ended the relationship with their ministry and my mentor. We remained friends outside the ministry, but I had a special relationship with him and his wife. As I joined a different church, I jumped right back into chaplaincy and continued but with a different group. This time, I went to the women's side of the jail. It was different, but I learned to adapt and was open for whatever God would teach me in the experience.

One Sunday afternoon I will never forget, while I was crossing the courtyard, I heard a voice. Now I know people question God's ability to speak to us or are angel's real or is the devil real? All I can say is when God speaks, those who have experienced it will tell you it is real, and you hear it. Your spirit certainly identifies with it on every level, and that did not just come out of your brain. His still small voice is plain and clear. I heard Oprah said, "It comes first in a whisper, well, it was clear, and it was not just a thought in my head." The voice said, "I am going to put you in the jail fulltime as a teacher." I stopped and looked around, laughed and said, "Yeah, right." I looked up and asked God how he was going to make that happen. At the time, I did not think this was odd because I got use to what I would call God's nudges. If you haven't experienced it, that's because you don't listen. The Holy Spirit of God guides and directs us on a daily basis." It is up to us to be still enough to hear the voice of the Holy Spirit. It's not a shout, but most time, a whisper. Something he will direct you by bring a scripture to your mind. I asked God the question of how would he do this, but I found I had to wait to for the answer. I never seem to figure out the set up until I am already walking in it.

As I mentioned earlier, I left my former church and joined another church. I was sent there to meet the person God would use to propel me into the mission of my next assignment. During meet and greet time, I introduced myself to a woman who I truly found to be a godsend. She just happened to be the CEO of a domestic violence counseling agency and homecare business. She invited me to her agency and later hired me part time to work as a receptionist. She asked if I was interested in learning the facilitation of groups, and I eagerly jumped at the chance to learn a new job skill. Now I was not aware in that moment how God was going to use all this. All I knew is that I was in the right place, doing the right thing.

During my facilitation training, I was told to sit silently and listen in the group. No one knew I too had suffered at the hands of men who were mentally, emotionally, and on occasion physically abusive. As I sat in group, I was listening to the men in that room justify why they abused their partners. This was difficult, and I was angered to hear them blame the victims for their crimes. At times, I wanted to be the spokesperson for every woman who had suffered at the hands of a man, yet I could not express how I was feeling. I had to control my outrage and pay attention to what I needed to glean from the experience. I learned a lot about myself and how I allowed my power to be taken by a man, many who did not love me. I came to the realization that God was using this platform for a twofold purpose. First, it was to equip me for the work ahead and to provide answers to my own questions about abuse. I now understood through the training and group experiences that I was not to blame, as my abusers made me feel. I was not responsible for their bad behavior. What I was responsible for was accepting it and not walking away sooner. I became a stronger and more confident woman as I continued to do the work.

My boss came to me. Once again, she asked if I would enter a program for substance abuse counseling, and I said yes. I started taking courses immediately and shortly after, I became an adult education teacher, providing services for inmates within a county jail programs. I guess you can see where this was going. Remember I said the voice of God said he was going to put me in the jail to teach. She introduced me to another student who also worked in the county jail. It turns out they both worked in the very jail that I ministered in over the last nine years. After meeting the two of them, my friend said the gentlemen I met had a position in his area of the agency. I spoke with him, and we set up an interview, and I was hired shortly after. You might say once again that it was a coincidence, but I say it was a setup. It had God's handprint all over it. When God is involved in it, most often it will lead you to the next big thing. Each experience lends itself to help you to develop a skill for the purpose, which God is calling you to.

My job in the jail started off small but helped me to get acclimated to the environment. The agency provided certain services for the inmates, and I would go to the different housing units of the jail. I was fortunate to have the opportunity to learn my way around the entire jail campus and meet the officers who work there. I did not know at the time where this was going, but my attitude was to show up and give it my best. After a year of working with the agency, my friend came to me and said she was going to quit the agency. I tried to talk her out of it, but her mind was made-up. She did just as she said and quit the following week. The agency came to me and asked if I would take over her classroom. In that moment, I was reminded of what God had spoken to me back when I was doing chaplaincy. I laughed and said to myself, "Never doubt God. If he said it, it will come to pass."

This was another lesson in faith, and it again confirmed to me that he keeps every promise. I was excited and felt inadequate at the same time. I thought to myself, *Teacher, I am not a teacher.* I heard in my spirit once again that God assured me, that he will send the helper the "Holy Spirit," who will teach me how to become the teacher. I was completely walking by faith on this, and I said yes. I will take the job, not to mention the better paid that went along with the position. That next week, I walked over to the women's side of the jail and entered the officer's area. I could see through the glass doors as the ladies start to observe my presence in the area. It was like entering into the ring for a fight. I felt like I was going in to do battle, and I was outnumbered by my opponents. Now I had gone into these areas before, but this time, I was the main attraction. They all had heard that their teacher left, and a new instructor was coming. So, their curiosity was understandable, especially in an environment that is so restrictive, and you are powerless.

The officers briefed me and checked to see if I had any items that was consider contraband. They wished me luck, and the door unlocked. You could hear the loud click as the release of the door indicated I was free to enter. As I walked in, I could hear their whispers as they sized me up. I played it cool like I had done this a million time. I said good morning, quickly moved toward my desk, dropped my belongings, and waited for a response. The ladies waited in their seats, and all eyes were on me now. I told myself, "You got this," and I knew in the moment I had to fake it. My success depended on me controlling the narrative. I had to appear I knew what I was doing so they would not sense the fear or feelings of inadequacy. My mind kicked into gear, and I quickly decided we would make our first day an introduction and getting-to-know-each-other session. I reacted on pure instinct, making them feel safe with me. That first week turned out better than I could have ever hoped for or imagined. I was pleased with how I just knew at every turn what to do, and I felt God's presence throughout my time working with those women. I was able to learn how to prepare lessons for the class each day, facilitate discussion, and set boundaries with the ladies. This prepared me for the next phase of God's plan for me.

During the course of that next year, I worked full-time and did evening classes. Life for me continued to shift, and I was meeting other instructors throughout the jail. I found out there was another agency on the men's side of the jail, teaching adult-ed programs. I was told I needed a teaching credential to work with them, so I started inquiring about the process to obtain getting the credential. I found the school I needed to enroll in and started the process of taking the necessary courses. I just felt it was meant for me to take this step.

God uses the good and the bad. After that second year of working with my agency, I was scheduled to take a day off, which was approved by my manager. Her supervisor told me I could not have the time off. I was upset to say the least. It was my birthday coming up, and I had plans to see Mya Angelo in San Francisco. I told the Manager that I had been working diligently, always on time, had not had a day off since I started, and I had plans. She would not listen to my plea for mercy and threaten to fire me if I did not come in. I felt

I was at a crossroad in this situation. This was a difficult decision I had to make, but I prayed and told God, "You know I have worked hard and was diligent in all my time there. I felt a peace come over me about the decision of leaving my job.

The day came that I had scheduled off, and I went to see Mya Angelo and had the best birthday ever. I admired her work for a long time, and I felt nothing could stop me from seeing her. My manager kept her promise and fired me. It was with okay. I knew God had something better for me.

A few weeks later, I ran into another person I knew who told me about a domestic violence agency not far from my home, and they were hiring. I had left my first part-time job in the DV field to take my full-time teaching job, so I quickly applied for the position. Once I was hired, I thought I would be facilitating groups again, and to my surprise, my manager asked if we could talk. I sat down, and he began to tell me about a new contract the agency got, and he asked me to be the person to go teach a domestic violence class outside the agency. Well, I have to tell you, get ready because I was not ready for this either. I was contracted to go back to the same jail I just left. Ha, I know, I thought the same thing. I said, "God, you are something else." It was like I was boomeranged right back to where I was called to be. So off I went, but this time, it was different. On my first day, I was taken to a very large room, and I could tell by the size of it, this was no small classroom. Someone from the program's office can and give me a roaster, and I was told I would be teaching a group of 120 men. "Oh, wow" was my reaction. What have I gotten myself into? Fear tried to set in, but the Holy Spirit whispered, "I will be with you. You can do this." That afternoon, as I walked down classroom row, I knew this would change my life, and my prayer was to bring change to the lives of every student I had the privilege to teach. I can truly say God used me to plant seeds in the hearts of those men, that would impact families throughout the jail in multiple locations. I left my position with the domestic violence agency after a year when the contract ended. I went on to work with another DV agency and got hired by the police department for a brief period. I felt in my spirit the police department was not the position I should remain in, so I gave my notice and left. I received a call to come in for an interview with the adult program at the jail I left earlier that year. After the interview, I left for a vacation and received a call, with the news I was being offered a full-time position. I was given the assignment to start a new program. Over the next six years, I developed an addiction program which helped many men and women receive early release as a result of their participation. During that time, the jail put out statistics which showed students from my program were ranked the highest number of students, with the lease recidivism of all the addiction programs in that jail. Judges came to visit my program on occasion to see what I was doing because they saw a difference in the students that came to court, who graduated from the Healing Opportunity Program Environment (HOPE) program. The men in my program actually helped me come up with the name of the program. I believed in involving my students in all aspects of the program. I was able to see many people recover from addiction and enter the workforce as counselors, helping others achieve sobriety. I mention my accomplishments not to brag on myself, but to speaks of how my dependence on God's direction led to a great outcome, as a result of my obedience to him. Those years brought me much joy, knowing I was fulfilling my purpose.

Section 14

A Journey of Lessons

For the past sixty-six years now, throughout this journey, I have had many ah-ha moments. I began to understand that wisdom could only be learned through the lessons of my failures and my successes. Change was and still is inevitable. As we get older, we will experience life in unexpected ways. I realize what we refuse to learn from others, life has a way of schooling us. The lessons are oftentimes based on how we approach every task. Mapping out plans is great, but know that sometimes situations change, and you could be in for a bumpy ride. When we are faced with challenges, faith is sometimes all you have. You don't know what you don't know. People often say. I wish I knew then what I know now. If you haven't said that yet, you will. My advice, is observe, listen, and learn from everything around you. Find people who have experience in any area you are trying to grow in. Older adults are more likely to have experience in failures, as well as success. They can share how they navigated through the obstacles and achieved their goals. Here are some lessons that helped shape my spiritual journey, and my hope is that you glean from my experience.

Lesson 1: Spiritual Blindness

When I look back to the beginning of my life, I was not aware of the lost condition of my soul. I had received a sentence of death because I was a sinner. I was not aware that one man's sin passed condemnation to all mankind. But wait, I was just a child, full of innocence and wonder. I look normal on the outside with all my fingers and toes, two legs, two arms, but I had a condition called spiritual blindness, but this condition was unknown to me. I was already condemned to eternal death, but how could this be? I was just a child. Yes, but another child came into the world who knew no sin and died for me. I had no idea of God or the history of Jesus's birth, dead, and resurrection. I did not understand that Adam and Eve's sin brought death to all of us. I was unaware what God expected or how I could change my destiny. I fell into the trap of focusing on earthly pleasure, instead of spiritual matters. The rat race of life had me stressing over success and making it, not knowing, if I would even see the next day. I was striving for what I could achieve here on earth while God was more concern with my eternal destiny. Valuing spirituality is the highest achievement one can have. It grounds us in everything we do. When we are spiritually balanced, we can better manage our thoughts, feelings, and emotions. The Holy Spirit helps us stay grounded, and we are able to make better decisions.

When I became spiritually aware of this, my focus shifted. I had to be born again. That was the only way to see eternal life. The moment I surrendered my life to Christ, it brought the feeling of joy, peace, and belonging. God is and continues to be greater than anything I have ever experienced. I now feel his love, forgiveness, and acceptance. That's priceless. Knowing he put his son on the cross for me is true love. I know no one can love me like the one who gave his life for me. He gave me my sight. As the old spiritual song says, "I was blind, but now I see."

Lesson 2: Parent Rules

I did not always want to follow the rules of my parents, but I later realized after having children why those rules were necessary. I learned that giving children a foundation at the beginning is absolutely essential. The Bible says, "Foolishness is bound up the heart of a child." If a parent does not have structure, teach children how to be kind, honest, hardworking, polite, and set boundaries for them. When children had no structure too often, we see them end up in prison or dead. Providing a spiritual foundation for children can equip them in knowledge that can carry them through difficult times. It exposes them to a connection with God, who can help them navigate through school, job, career choice, and much more. I am so happy today that my parents modeled faith in my life, which was the greatest legacy they could have ever left for me. Yes, like most people, I wish they had left a big financial inheritance too, but I might have missed learning the ethics of hard work. They gave me a future of the eternal wealth, which is more valuable; something money can't buy. All that you see here in the earth will one day pass away. What we do here for Christ will remain and will be rewarded in eternity.

The Bible says to obey your parents and wear their instruction around your neck like a wreath. I followed my parent's rules when I was there, but later my rebellious ways brought certain hardships that taught me living a life of self-well was not the wises choice. God is my Father, and I am beholding to my parents for my faith. I made the mistake of thinking I was calling the shots over my life. It is foolish to think that we can stand against God. We cannot control, even the next breath we take. God and him alone has that control. That is deep if you think about it. I came to realize that I was in control over one thing, choosing to accept or reject what Christ did for me when he died on the cross.

I realized my today did not guarantee my tomorrow, and I can go one step further. When I see how many people whose life is cut short by an unexpected accident or they tragically become a victim of violence or die of an illness, I realized that could have been me. Life can slip away at anytime, anywhere, and there is nothing I or any of us could do to stop it from occurring. I use to hear people say, "We make plans, and God laughs." Well, it took me a while to chew on that thought, but I finally realized what they were saying. God truly is in control of life and the place where my soul will be in eternity. Who would sign up for suffering or death? The fact that we are born and then we die demonstrates our limitations. There is something bigger than us. I understood I do not call all the shots, and my very existence is a miracle every day. I recognize God is the power greater than myself, who is the giver of life and holds all power over all that exist.

Lesson 3: God's Reality

Seeing my baby sister change in an instant at the most difficult time of her life was the first glimpse I got of God. At the time, it did not seem like a big deal, but even then, God was revealing his presence to me. Making the connection of my sister's last few months on earth was a revelation that was unexpected and transformative. I realized God was coming up close and personal. Death has a way of getting our attention like nothing else. Losing her caused me to think on the afterlife scenario. I pictured her in heaven. I just knew, after witnessing her spiritual transformation, she could only be with God. I wanted to be sad about her passing, yet I couldn't help but question if I would ever see her again. I had heard when you die, you would reconnect with those who had gone on before you. Suddenly, the question of if God was real started to turn from a maybe to I believe. I didn't think losing my sister at age thirteen was fair, but who was I to question why she had to die. I was not the giver of her life, neither could I make the decision for her to live. Acceptance was my lesson when it came to her departure from this earth, and the reality of God's power came to me in full view. I understand the Bible's explanation of our human existence, so I no longer questioned life nor death. I believe God has a purpose and a reason for everything that happens. We may not understand it, but that does not matter in the larger scheme of things. None of us have control over when or where our lives will end.

The Bible has transformed me, given me a deeper understanding of its principles. It truly is a divine book. The power of Holy Spirit who was sent to be our teacher and guide truly exists for every believer. Those of us who have experienced the divinity of God know what we have experienced is real. Just as I myself in times past and was in a place where this was hidden from my existence. I too would have questioned all of this, but because I had many supernatural experiences, that deepened my understanding of God and continued to help me hold on to hope. He is real to me, and I believe eternity is in my future. I believe that Jesus died for me. That his dead paid the price for my sins. If you want to know if any of what I am saying is true, all you have to do is pray to him and see if he will come closer than you ever would imagine.

> "Ask and it will be given to you, seek and you will find: Kock and the door will be opened to you" (Matthew 7:7).
>
> "For, everyone that calls upon the name of the Lord will be saved" (Romans 10:13).

Lesson 4: Youthful Experiences Can Shape Your Future

I did not realize in those days how the foundation that was laid in my youth shaped the trajectory of my future. I learned that the family I grow up in played a vital role in shaping the view of who I was and who I could become. I can tell you they were not the most encouraging bunch. My mother's emotional unavailability impacted how I dealt with men. I attracted men who too were emotionally unavailable. I sought attention from men who were abusive like the brothers I grew up with. I had no relationship with my birth father most of my life, which I understood gave me an attitude that a man was not necessary. However, at the age of seven years old, God sent us my stepfather, who was the bright light, who I believe God sent to offset the negativity around me. But the first six years are critical for a child's development. The damage had already been done. People I interacted with throughout my younger years all provided positive or negative beliefs. The lesson here is your past does not have to continue to dominate your future. There is a way to disrupt the old beliefs and develop new beliefs. My study of psychology was the saving grace, I needed. I understood how the family of organ created patterns of behaviors and beliefs which affected how I acted. The mind is a powerful thing. Thoughts control behavior, yet you can reshape those thoughts of defeat to thoughts of success. Even though darkness is all around the light of hope is always in the distance.

Seek wisdom. If I can encourage anyone reading my story to stop, look, and listen, wisdom is yelling for you to seek its path. I never understood the importance of seeking wisdom. Who talks about this? No one in the circle of people I encountered. The Bible has a lot to say about wisdom and is the only place I found it spoken about, not in daily conversation. I was void of understanding and made foolish choices. I thought I was grown enough to leave my parents as seventeen. I wanted to be in control of my life without them interfering, but later realized I still needed guidance. Talk to people who have live for a while, their experiences can save you from a lot of heartache. When you're young, you have this thought, "Oh well, that was your experience, but for me, it will be different." Let me tell you, there is nothing new under the sun. If I tried it and it did not work, more than likely you will have the same result too.

> "The fear of the Lord is the beginning of knowl-
> edge, but fools despise wisdom and instruction"
> (Proverbs 1:7).

> "Do not forsake wisdom and she will protect you,
> love her and she will watch over you" (Proverbs
> 4:6).

Ask for help. I finally understood that I needed to stop and ask for help. I didn't have to know it all. It was okay to ask others to counsel me on things I was not wise enough to navigate through. Even if you're an adult, you too can look to others. I learned that we do not always get what we need when we are younger, and it is okay, as long as you are willing to ask others around you for help when you need it. Getting help from people who have been where your trying to go is wise. Everyone will need help, and if it cannot come from those in your immediate circle, go outside of the circle. Don't be afraid to share your thoughts, feelings, and struggles with someone you trust. There is an old saying, "No man is as island." Simply put we are not meant to be alone, and we should not isolate ourselves from others. It leads to depression, drinking, drugs, and sadly suicide for some. Many young adults have taken this path. They may have felt alone and thought they had no one who understood or whom they could trust with their pain.

We do not always have family members that we can turn to, but my church family was the closest thing to my birth family. I found relationships with other believers, which became a safe place to develop lasting relationships. I had the opportunity to be a part of many Bible study groups or what we call life groups. The people I have met over the years were not perfect, but I too was not perfect. We all had something in common; we were all seeking to be better people. We all shared in the common bond of trusting God. Our spiritual experience was shared with great joy, and we encouraged one another throughout our journeys. The church plays a vital role in my life, and I had no regret in coming to know God's mercy, forgiveness, and love for me. My adolescent and young adult life showed me how much I need God. He helps me navigate through the good and the bad of life. He has gifted me in many ways, and I hope to use those gifts to be a blessing to others. I realized my purpose and understood he had a plan for me.

Power of prayer: I learned about prayer in childhood. My family valued prayer, and all of us learned to believe God was there, and he would hear us when we call upon him. I learned the power of prayer as a way for coping with life challenges and disappointment. I could cry out to God when no one else was around. Having others pray for you and with you is powerful. The bible says, When two stands in agreement on anything that you ask, it shall be done for them of the father which is in heaven. People sometimes think there is a certain formula for the way you pray. Prayer is simply talking to God. Telling him how you feel, not just asking him for things. When you express thanks, or praise him for his goodness or singing a song, it is all okay. Building a relationship is the key. Prayer is not just a time when troubled situation come, but when everything is well too. Giving thanks to God at all times, the scripture says, is God's desire. We praise him in the good times, as well as the bad. Prayer can bring joy and be a place of comfort for the present and our hope for tomorrow.

> "For I know the plans I have for you, declares the Lord, plans to prosper you and not to harm you, plans to give you a hope and a future" (Jeremiah 29:11).

Lesson 5: Not for Sissies

Adulthood is defiantly not for the faint of heart. It pushed me out of my comfort zone and demanded that I grow up. When I left home too early with no plan, no money in the bank and no clue how I would make ends meet; the realities of life slapped me silly. I had a job at sixteen, but in no way was I making enough money to step out on my own. By the grace of God, I was fortunate to have parents who trained me to be responsible. They did not give us whatever we wanted or bought us the latest gadgets or let us lay around the house till we felt like getting up. We have a routine each day that required us to participate in the daily functions of the home. As responsible members of our household, we learned to do laundry, cook, and work in the garden. From the time our feet hit the floor, we ran around making our beds, cleaning the house, waxed floors, washed walls, or doing whatever other task our parents expected of us. My second job was school, but after school, we were required to come straight home and make sure our chores were all completed before playtime began.

The lessons of hard work paid off, and I was able to apply all the values my parents instilled in me. I knew instinctively how I to fend for myself. I had the drive I needed to make it in this world. I would not say it was always easy, but I had the tenacity to stick with the challenges and meet obstacles head on. I learned to fight harder to accomplish my goals. My life could have been different if my parents did not push me, but it was the push that made me who I became. I just wanted to be out of my parent's house and away from their rules, yet I had no idea how challenging it would be to be an adult. I was not very teachable back then, and my stubbornness made my path rocky. It was not the easiest or the best launch into adulthood.

The lesson here—be careful what you wish for and do not think you know it all. Even as an adult, it is wise to remain teachable. Find good mentors and talk through your plans. Ask them questions that will make the path a little smoother, having gain wisdom and insight into what could be the possible pitfalls. Life will throw you curve balls, and if you are not equipped with the mental and spiritual fortitude to handle those curve balls, you will be overwhelmed. Being connected to a power greater than yourself is pivotal and holds the key to success. When you are spiritually grounded, it gives you a different perspective. It took me years to come to the knowledge of this fact, but you do not have to wait as long as I did. God is waiting for you.

Lesson 6: Seeking the Father's Face

Up to this point in my life, I never believed that people were inherently evil or bad. Although this experience was unexpected and scary, I learned that not everyone had my best interest at heart. I never understood how another person's agenda could put me put in harm's way. I was naive and wanted to think the best about people. I was happy I was not injured or molested in the situation. After experiencing an attempt of sexual assault to actually being sexually assaulted, I realized these events brought me closer to God. Now I am not saying I needed this type of misfortunate occurrences to find God, but I am saying God used these situations to change my heart so I would have a greater desire and want to draw nearer to him. It was his love and grace that turned it around for my good. He promises us he will take the bad and turn it around for our good. The lesson here whether in times of trouble or when all is going will in your life it is important to know you can call upon him and he hears your concerns. If you are a believer of God, then having a relationship with him is not just going to church or asking him for things or visiting church a few times a year. Interaction with God is the one thing that you should seek to run toward daily. It is perfecting your desire for his presence and the knowledge of his will for your life. You converse with him, you listen to him, and you share your deepest concerns. We often make time for those we love. Well, God desires our attention as well. He is seeking to share an intimate space with us. There is a verse of scripture in the book of Matthew 7:23–24, "Jesus said, that on the day of judgement, many will say to me, Lord, Lord, did we not prophesy in your name, and performed many miracles in your name? Then I will say, depart from me you workers of iniquity, I never knew you." Simple means we cannot have hypocrisy in our relationship with God. He knows us, but he wants us to know him. He is very explicit in wanting our worship, our praise, and us actively sharing our faith. He asks us to draw closer to him, and he promises to draw closer to us. The relationship should be a give and take relationship. Let me share with you that we come out on the better end because he is God and has no need of what we have to offer, but his love for us drives him to bring goodness and mercy into our lives.

> "Then you will call upon Me and go and pray to Me, I will listen to you. And you will seek Me and find Me, when you search for Me with all you heart" (Jeremiah 29:12–13).

Lesson 7: The Great Deceiver

Scripture tell us "the god of this world has blinded the minds of the unbelievers, to keep them from seeing the light of the gospel of the glory of Christ, who is the image of God" (2 Corinthians 4:4). I found this to be certainly true for my life. I learned that my inability to understand and know God was due to spiritual blindness. The light of Christ was shown through the power of the Holy Spirit. We walk in darkness until the truth of Jesus Christ is revealed. Why? Because the great deceiver is still pulling the wool over the eyes of unbelievers and hardening their hearts toward God.

We have an enemy who we cannot see. At least not with our naked eye, we need spiritual eyes. Our enemy comes in many forms and have many disguises. His name is Satan. It was told to us from the Bible that Satan was first called the dragon who started war against Michael and his angels. This same mind-set was passed onto us. He lives among us, walking around as a roaring lion, seeking who he may devour, as the scripture tells us (1 Peter 5:8). We no longer should wonder why there is so much evil in the world. The God of this world is alive and well. When we decide we don't need God, and we say, "I will" just as Satan did, we make the decision to denounce him as our creator. Wake up, people, we too are in jeopardy of eternal damnation. Satan's day is coming, when Jesus will return to earth and the last battle will be fought before his is cast into eternal darkness. We can't see or understand this without the power of God's Holy Spirit living in us. The Holy Spirit is our seal that we have been approved by God to receive eternal life. The scripture says, "In him, you also, after listening to the message of truth, the gospel of your salvation—having also believed, you were sealed with the Holy Spirit of promise, who is the guarantee of our inheritance until we acquire possession of it, to the praise of his glory" (Ephesians 1:13–14). This is God's promise to all believers, and without that seal, we will not see God. Satan is fighting for your eternal soul. So, if he can whisper or guide you into rebelling against God, he will. He wants to destroy as many souls as possible because he knows his days are numbered. Confess Christ today.

Lesson 8: Believe What You Cannot See

This lesson came on the heels of all my failures. It was hard to believe what I could not see. Like so many of you, I thought if I cannot see it, then it must not exist. That mind-set is not deliberately taught but is kind of an unspoken rule that we oftentimes lived by. Remember the old saying, "I'm from the show-me state." Well, that mind-set did not work well in my life. I had to come to the belief that the God of the universe was real. God, for some reason, decided he would show me just how real he really was. In my arrogance, as one of his creation, I had the audacity to think I knew better of what was good for my life than him. What a joke. When I think back on the pride and the ignorance that flooded my brain throughout those years and when I look at how vast the universe are and the power of God's hand to have created it all, I am humbled. I know now he is God, the only true and living God. Doubt left my mind a long time ago. God has demonstrated his power in my life in ways that sometimes it's unbelievable. The fact that he protected me when others tried to harm me. He helped me come to my senses when I was making crazy choices. He provided financially in miraculous ways. No one could ever convince me that my God does not exist. It is too late because I am a believer. God will reveal himself to anyone who dare to believe. I can tell you that he is real, but I would leave you with this tip, call on him, and you can experience him for yourself. When you confess Jesus Christ died for your sin and believe that God raised him from the dead, the Bible assures us we will be saved. The assurance of eternal life with God is only one aspect of faith, but the relationship is ongoing. Walking with him day by day is quite miraculous. I encourage you to believe what you cannot see. That's called faith.

Lesson 9: Every Knee Must Bow

This biblical term taken from the Bible was literally true for my life. When I came back to Christ, I was in a bowed position. Know this, I was broken, bruised from the dysfunction and pain I suffered. My mind was wrecked and full of regret for the time I spent chasing sin. I was humiliated and discussed with trusting all the wrong people. There was nowhere else to go but down on my knees and ask God to help me manage my life. I humbled myself before him and trusted that he was the only resource I needed to bring my life back to sanity. This was the first step it took for me to see true change. I could see why the big book of AA says this is the first step. Humility is huge with God. Pride is repulsive to God. He says that pride always goes before a fall. He is so right. I saw it in my life over and over again. Until I was able to admit I was in need of a savior, the savior Jesus Christ, I continued on the path of destruction. I have no problem today being honest with what God already knows about me. He knows every wrong thought, every evil desire, and every sinful act I committed in the past, as well as those of the future. As the scriptures says, God will forgive all my sins, but I must continue to confess my sins.

> "If we claim to be without sin, we lie and the
> truth is not in us. If we claim we have not sinned,
> we make him a liar, but if we confess our sins, he
> is faithful and just to forgive us" (1 John 1:8–10).

In addition to getting God's forgiveness for me, I understood how much of that forgiveness would hinge on how I have forgiven others. Repentance is a continuous act in my life because of my sin nature. The Apostle Paul said it best. He said, "So I discovered this principle: When I want to do what is good, evil is with me" (Romans 7:21 HCSB). Paul called this the sin of the flesh. Which means as long as I live in the body, I am naturally inclined to sin. Know this is frustrating, but at least I know why I react to people or things negatively with all the best intentions, I miss the mark. That's again why Jesus came.

Lesson 10: Transformation

The process of change for all believers is gradual. I learned it will continue for the rest of my life. I had to practice patience with myself and others. Becoming a Christian, it doesn't mean we become perfect people. Quite the contrary, we find ourselves agreeing with God that we are sinners and in need of a savior. God gives us, the power to want to change, but that change is a day-to-day process. We can't accomplish this in our own strength. The Word of God is our instruction for how we transition into the image of Christ. Christ wants us to follow in his footsteps, not to suffer crucifixion as he suffered death on a cross, but a spiritual crucifixion. This means pulling away from one's fleshly desires. Taking on holiness, instead of striving for superficial things of this world. He said, "In order to follow me, one must dye to himself." A believer should not be living a self-absorbed life. It is not all about what I want and how I want it, I have to seek God's will in the process of making all my decisions. A higher purpose could mean I seek to serve others and use my resources to give to the poor. Mother Theresa was a perfect example of a person who dedicated her life to helping others. Have you made a decision to transform your life and be a servant of God?

In order to transform, I had to be willing to go through a radical change in a variety of ways. This first is understanding that my thoughts were not God's thoughts, and my ways were not his ways. I learned how I thought about myself and others were quite misguided. This world perverts our beliefs and robs us of our innocence. I realized my mind was being shaped by distorted views of culture and what I saw in social media. Transformation of my mind and spirit was imperative for my life to soar to new heights. The Bible says, "Do not be conformed to the pattern of this world," so I had to take steps to redirect my thoughts, as well as my behaviors. Here are five steps that helped me in my journey.

Step 1—I asked God to guard and redirect my mind. The mind is the place of intellect, reasoning, and intentions. All behavior stems from the mind, so transformation is impossible when we lack the skills to control our thoughts. If my thoughts are misaligned, so is my behavior, and this can prove to be fatal. Just saying a simple prayer, asking God to guide and direct my thoughts, helps me to start my day on a positive note. Showing gratitude for what I have and not being focused on the things I don't have, which refocuses my energy in the right direction. Gratitude gives hopes and dreams for a brighter tomorrow.

"Finally, brothers and sisters, whatever is true, whatever is noble whatever is right, whatever is pure, whatever is lovely, whatever is admirable— if anything is excellent or praiseworthy—think about such things. Whatever you have learned or received or heard from me, or seen in me, put it into practice. And the God of peace will be with you" (Philippians 4:8–9).

God encouraged me to think on the good in life. When I actively put my mind on things above as the scriptures says, I find I am able to focused on God and not on all the troubles of this world. I learned God's ways, are to treat others as I want to be treated. The concept is however you want people to treat you, in any situation, is the same way you should treat other people. Whether it is a family member, spouse, friend, neighbor, or strangers, you don't know. The lesson is, if you do this for others, it will be done unto you. This again is a spiritual principle that we don't always identify as essential. I have learned this is especially difficult in a marital relationship. Seeking my partner's interest above my own has been an eye-opening challenge that God commands of us. I can't say I get it right every time, but this is what I am striving to do. Loving another person is especially problematic when two people see each other's faults. We tend to put conditions on how we love them, yet God loves us unconditionally, despite our faults. We, too, are encouraged in scripture to do the same. In addition to loving others, serving others is equally important. God wants to use our time, talent, and our resources to accommodate others. Whether you lend a hand to someone in need of help, or taking the time to listen to a person during a stressful moment, making yourself available to others is what God desires for us to do. Jesus came to serve, and he asked me to do the same.

Step 2—*Recognize the source of self-focused and self-defeating thoughts.* I am challenged daily to evaluate thoughts and behaviors that do not reflect God's character. God declares that the mind must be renewed daily because he knows this is the place that is most vulnerable. Remember when Satan came to Eve, he told her to not believe what God had said but place in her mind a lie. He was able to redirect her obedience toward God. He gave her a new thought, which in turn changed the course of history. That one moment of weakness took her to a path of death. Let's not forgot Eve repeats the lie to Adam, and he too choses to disobey God. God understood the power of a misguided thoughts. Adam and Eve held the fate of all humanity. That same lie about who God is and what he has said continues to be perpetrated by the demonic forces around us. We are literally in a spiritual battle every day. We don't see it, and we don't recognize that the adversary of our soul still uses the same tactics. Nothing has changed; his tricks are the same. He knows if he can win on the playing field of our mind, he can destroy any dream, any gifts, or any chance for us to succeed at anything we attempt. If you have felt held back, fearful to move forward, check out what thoughts you may be engaged in. Positive thoughts bring positive results, while negative thoughts bring negative results. Never underestimate the power of thoughts.

> "Casting down imaginations and every high thing that exalts itself against the knowledge of God, and bringing into captive every thought to the obedience of Christ" (2 Corinthians 10:5).

Step 3—Replacing self-focused thinking with a God-focused mind-set. Focusing on God requires me to take time and make the effort to put God in the forefront of my thinking. When I awake, I start by setting my mind on Christ. Each day, I think of the love and forgiveness God has for me and the grace he gives to me every day. I thank him for life, breath, health, and the bed I had to sleep in. Praising the father and giving glory to God is important. Giving honor to him refocuses my mind. If I allow negative thinking to creep in, I become cynical. I become critical toward others, selfish, which later develops into self-absorbed behaviors. Someone once said, "Look at the word *sin*. In the middle, you see the I. The I represents the obsession we have with ourselves. I thought that was pretty clever, given it holds a lot of true about the human condition. If we as a people were focused on someone else other than ourselves, we could change the world. The call of every believer is to have the mind of Christ. In the book of Romans 12:2, Paul tell us that the only way we can be transformed is by renewing our mind. The renewal is done by reading God's Word. When his thoughts become our thoughts, then we will be able to know what God's will is—his good, pleasing, and perfect will the bible says. This was Christ's attitude. He came to give his life for all to demonstrate what an act of love will do. Christ came to serve and not to be served. Reading the Bible each day or meditating on a verse of scripture helps me to yield to God. It helps me to seek peace with all men, especially those who do not look like me or believe what I believe. The Holy Spirit helps me to extend forgiveness to those that may hurt me or give mercy to those who may not deserve it. Each day, I can choose how I think, which then propels me to do positive things.

> "If then you have been raised with Christ seek the things that are above, where Christ is, seated at the right hand of God. Set your minds on things that are above, not on things that are in the earth" (Colossians 3:1–2).

Step 4—Rest in the truth that you are accepted in Jesus Christ. Resting in God's truth *is* an important part of the process. It helps me combat the negative beliefs about who I am and who's I am. Through faith in Christ, I can have peace with God. He calls me his own and tells me I am never alone. He promises he will never leave me or forsake me. I feel his presence and have faith that he will keep that promise. He gives me hope for eternity, and although I know I deserve hell, he promises everlasting life. Jesus took the death that I deserved, and I am forever grateful for what he did for me. You too can have that assurance if you put your faith in Jesus Christ.

Step 5—Repeat steps 1 to 4 daily. Living a transformed life requires having a routine. Many people seek quiet meditation, Bible reading, long walks, yoga, or some form of practice to quite their mind. Whatever you choose, I hope you include God in the process.

Lesson 11: Serving Others Is the Highest Calling

I am convinced that everyone is born with a gift or talent that is uniquely special for the purpose of serving others. I never wanted to teach, and yet my role as a teacher was the only job I loved. Although I had many other skills and talents, I know I was called to teach to evoke change. I shared in my story on how God called me to the jail as a teacher. Although I was unsure of the outcome, I stepped out on faith, and God directed my path. He used my life for fifteen years in county jails to impact those suffering from addiction and abuse. I had no idea what God could do through me, but he used my life to help others. I give all the praise to God because at that time I lacked the confidence and skill, yet one act of faith propelled me into a successful career. God saw something greater in me than I was able to see in myself. Lives were transformed, and I saw many families impacted because of an act of me choosing to believe God. How many lives could you impact if you too step out on faith and allow God to direct you toward your purpose and the opportunity to serve others in your local community.

My service in the church is another my way of participating in God's mission. He tells us to love, to give, to serve, and to get involved in activities that has opportunities which benefit the lives of others. We are also called to share the gospel of Christ with others. Serving has brought me great joy and peace. Helping other people takes the focus off ourselves and is an act of love. God commands each of us to love others and treat them as you would like them to treat you. I truly understand that my life is not my own, but by God's design, I came into the world to be used of God for whatever purpose he puts in front of me. Uplifting another person is the best thing any of us can do. If you have never volunteered your time, given money to a homeless person, or shown compassion to a total stranger or friend, then I recommend you try it.

> "Greater love has no one than this to lay down one's life for one's friends" (John 15:13 NIV).

> "Whoever is kind to the poor lends to the Lord, and he will reward them for what they have done" (Proverbs 19:17).

I found that becoming a Christian was not the only step in following Christ. I learned accepting Christ was only the beginning of my journey as a believer. Jesus called me to follow his lead and get involved in the mission, just as the disciples did. Jesus told his disciples to be fishers of men. I now was being called to build the church and become a witness of the good news. Church attendance is only to be unified with other believers, who, too, share in God's purpose and plan to reach all nations with the message of Jesus Christ. Jesus said, "Take up your cross and follow me." That is a command for all believers. These points are found in the book of Matthew 16:24–26 (ESV). It says, "Jesus told his disciples, 'If anyone would come after me, let him deny himself and take up his cross and follow me. For whoever would save his life will lose it, but whoever loses his life for my sake, will find it. For what will it profit a man, if he gains the whole world and forfeits his soul? Or what shall a man give in return for his soul?'" Reading this helped me to understand that my life had a deeper mission. I was not just called on by God for the purpose of salvation, but for his higher purpose, which meant I have to give my life to do his will and seek the lost and save others. I love God; his mission should be important to me as it is to him. The keys are given in scripture.

Part 4

My Understanding of Faith

Reading the Bible brought clarity as I watched God take me on a journey in which he introduced himself and became as a loving father. He pursued me, even as I made many poor choices, and yet he did not give up on me. He demonstrated his love, protection, provision, and favor in my life even when I did nothing to deserve his faithfulness. There are many scriptures that spoke of God's pursuit of me. Here are a few examples of scripture that stood out to me. In the book of Jeremiah 31:3, God declares his love for Israel in this passage. "I have loved you with an everlasting love; I have drawn you with unfailing kindness." God's love for his people was so great; he delivered them from their enemies and the oppressors who held them captive. Here is another example which says, "For it is God who works in you both to will and to do for *His* good pleasure" (Philippians 2:13 NKJV). This passage let me know he was already working to change my circumstance. I watched my parents professed their belief in God, as they were devoted churchgoers who never missed a Sunday, but behind the scene of all this, God was orchestrating his plan for my life using my parents as conduits to set the foundation for my faith. When I think about how big that is, it humbles me. Why would God call little old me? Imagine the Creator of the universe looking among billions of people he created, and he chooses you? Wow, just saying that gives me chills. Another scripture that confirms this concept is, "There is none who understands; there is none who seeks after God" (Romans 3:11 NKJV). I was one of those who did not seek after God, but nonetheless, God loved me enough to call me. Jesus said, "No one can come to me unless the Father who sent me draws him, and I will raise him to life on the last day" (John 6:44 ISV). Lastly, my favorite is in the book of Jeremiah, which says, "For I know the plans I have for you, declares the LORD, plans to prosper you and not to harm you, plans to give you hope and a future" (Jeremiah 20:11 NIV).

For many years, I chose to deny God's existence simply because I could not see him, and yet God said the very proof of his existence is seen in creation. The apostle Paul wrote, "For since the creation of the world, God's invisible attributes, his eternal power and divine nature, have been understood and observed by what he made, so that people are without excuse." Oh snap, I have no excuse not to believe nature speaks of his existence? I don't know about you but passages like this was a wake-up call for me (Romans 1:20 ISV). I truly believe the question of faith comes up for every human soul. How I chose to respond was my responsibility. I realized denying him had an eternal consequence. Just as I believe heaven is real, I also believe those who deny him will be eternally separated from him.

I fell into the mindset of the world, thinking my success was based on education and how much money was in my bank account. No one ever told to me that life is full of unexpected twist and turns. No one told me that heartache was inevitable, and painful events will happen. I did not understand that the promise of a happy and blissful life was not guaranteed. They did not tell me that disappointment, heartbreak, sadness, depression, sickness, pain, grief, loss, and death are all a part of the human experience. These are realities parents do not talk about, but life has its own way of waking us up to the truth.

Suffering brought me to my knees, and then I had to look up toward the heavens for God to take away my suffering. I was at my lowest point of brokenness before I surrendered to God. When I came to the end of my efforts, then and only then I was able to experience the pure love that only God brings. No matter how long it took for me surrender to God, his love for me never wavers. He showed me he had always been there, just waiting for me to call upon him. Despite my rebellious heart, he gave his Son, Jesus Christ, as a ransom for my sin. His unconditional love for mankind causes him to forgive, show kindness, and demonstrate patience when I blow it.

I wanted to share about the hope that lies within me. I wrote this book so others who may feel hopeless, who may feel they have been dealt a bad hand can understand; God is for you and not against you. When all has failed in your life, be encouraged that God wants the best for you too. He is waiting with open arms, not to commend you but to give you a future and great hope.

Today life is different for me. I do not fear where I will spend eternity. I believe I have been born again, and Christ has become my righteousness. He paid the price for my sin, and the gift of eternal life is real to me. I believe I will be saved from the eternal darkness of hell. I praise him because he has shown me his love is unconditional. He has been the provider as he promised. I now experience joy, and I feel his peace each day. I am truly grateful he revealed himself to me and took the fear away. Now I know him to be a loving father who is always there. I know I can call upon him in good and bad times.

The day I close my eyes in death. I will be at peace because I will be in the house of the Lord for all eternity. As I move toward the hope of his promise to know I have done all I could do to obey God's purpose for my life, I want to hear, "Well done, my good and faithful servant, come into my kingdom." My spirit has truly bore witness of his spirit. Living with faith has given me a different perspective of my role in society. I have purpose and know God has a plan for me. My existence has a deeper meaning, and I don't feel like I am here to merely exist.

I don't beat myself up anymore, but I strive to do better. The scripture tells me I am not alone in the work of God transforming me into the image of Christ. He is working in me to accomplish every good work. He also says to press on toward the mark of the high calling of God. I find comfort in knowing my success and strength is achieved with Him. I also understand I can't do it without Him. I learned my spirit is willing, but my flesh is weak. I understanding the battle to do good is one we all have to fight. Scripture really opens your eyes to know what makes us fall back into evil desires or why we fail to love others as ourselves. So please know that Christ is the only one who knew no sin, which makes his death significant. I will need to call on him and pray for his power to keep me focused on the higher purposes in life. Prayer and repentance is a daily practice for me. I recommend being thankful at all times. Having gratitude for even the smallest things in life can bring great joy. You can always find others who may be suffering worse than you. Gratitude should not be measured by your successes, but by the quality of being thankful, and a readiness to show appreciation for and to return kindness. The fact that I have breath each day is enough for me to be grateful.

Our Story

I didn't want to leave out the best part of my story and tell you all where I am today. After having the experience of prior failed relationships, including a four-year marriage that ended in divorce, I prayed to God and said I was going to wait after the failed marriage. I was willing to wait for God's provision for a husband like everything else God provided for my life. I read a scripture that says, "Because of the temptation of sexual immorality, each man should have his own wife and each woman her own husband" (1 Corinthians 7:2). After reading that passage it was plain to me, what the will of God was concerning marriage. I believed he would provide a God-fearing man who was faithful in his belief and willing to serve other people. I kept my focus on God's business, the business of ministering to people in jails and prison and the business of affecting change in the lives of the students who came to my recovery program. I was reminded of scripture where Jesus said, "I was in prison and you came to me." I want my life to be used to reflect God's compassion and mercy toward those going through troubled time. This was my calling; this was the place God called me to have the most impact in the world.

Who knew being obedient and following the spirit's leading would take me to the man who would be my husband. He too had been previously married but chose to wait before choosing another wife.

I met him after enrolling into a drug and alcohol course in which a woman, whom I befriended, was the instrument God used to bring my husband and I together. Without telling the whole entire story, she was a coworker of my husband, which I was not aware of when we met. She was in the Jehovah Witness faith, and I was sharing my faith with her quite often. Little did I know, so was the man I would marry. Neither of us knew this would be the very reason we would meet. She begged me to meet him, telling me what a nice guy he was, explaining we had common interest. We both pushed the idea of meeting away for six months. Our lives were focused on our work in school and church ministry. What we didn't know was the first semester of school, he and I were in the same class and never met or spoke to each other. Her persistence to get us together was somewhat humorous because of how persistent she was. I was so sick of her telling me how great he was, but I was curious about him. He too was being told he should meet me, and we had things in common. She was speaking of our faith. We were very unaware of it at the time. Her persistence drove us to say yes. She would tell me, "You don't have to marry him, just meet him." I thought what would be the harm, and if it would stop her from nagging me about him, why not?

We both gave in at the same time and agreed to meet by phone. Back then, pagers were popular, so I put my number and his pager, and he returned the call. He was very pleasant as we continued to talk for some weeks, and he asked if we could meet for lunch. I was reluctant, but my curiosity got the best of me. I agreed to meet him at his job. When I arrived, he was not on site, so I waited in my car. As I sat there, I saw him walking up the street and realized, he was someone I saw in class during my first semester of the program. My first reaction was, "Oh no, not that guy! He is the guy from my class." I wanted to duck, but there was nowhere to hide. It was too late. He came over to my car to confirm who I was. He asked if I would come in so he could finish a task he left undone earlier. I agreed and followed him in. Once inside the courtyard, I heard many of the clients calling my name, and it was apparent we shared the same clients. I worked with them in the jail program and the clients did outpatient addiction treatment with my husband. We were surprised at the this but made the connection that God was doing something in both of our lives. I witnessed too many of these clients, and after their release he led many to a confession of their faith in Christ. We understood we were working as a team, and that was the thing that sparked our relationship's interest. I prayed for a God-fearing man with the gift of evangelism. I went so far as to ask God to make sure he was at least six feet. Well, he was six two. There is a verse in the Bible that says, "Let your request be made known and another that says, 'whatever you ask, believe and you shall receive.'" Now I know that doesn't mean we ask for the ridiculous, but I do believe if our motives are pure in what we ask, God would honor our request.

We are coming upon our twentieth anniversary and, like most couples, have had to learn about each other. We have gone through many highs and lows. My husband suffered through cancer treatment, but praise God, he's doing great. I know we will have other challenges because suffering is a part of the human experience. The great thing in having a life partner is you know that you don't have to go through tough times alone. Not only do we have one another, but we have a great church community that stands with us and the fellowship of other believers. Our Christian brothers and sisters are very important to us. They are our extended family who share in the good times and the hard time. We appreciate each and every one of them.

As I am coming upon sixty-eight years of age, it is my hope to continue to run my race with as much energy as possible. I don't want to slow down throughout the remainder of my years on the earth. I want to explore new possibilities for ministry, helping through volunteer work, or doing my art or writing. Today I have hope and faith to continue my journey, leaving the legacy of joy, peace, and most importantly, *love*.

Life in Ministry

Our life in the church is very important to us. We grow in our understanding of Christ's mission to reach the lost and provide a safe environment to thrive. No matter what we are doing, it's always a good time with our sisters and brothers in Christ. We absolutely love working alongside each other, encouraging one another. We are family, and the bonds we share are unbreakable. Whether we are serving in ministry at our church, feeding the homeless, doing community work in our local schools, or spending time in our life groups, these are the moments I cherish and will always remember. Church has made our lives richer and fills our hearts with joy, hope, and happiness. No one has to be alone in the world because you can find family everywhere you look. We have attended marriage retreats for the past eighteen years to keep our relationship growing stronger. We have been supported by the people around us who continue walking in faith with us and remind us of the importance of loving one another. I will never forget how my life have grown and transformed because of the people God has placed in my life.

Meet the Family

My father is on the far left of this photo. He and his brothers were men faith, and although not perfect, they were the leaders of the legacy of my faith. I honor them for the seeds of faith, which was planted in my childhood. My birth father was a man who believed in God, and the foundation he instilled in me as his daughter is still alive many years later. He followed God's call to lead his children in the way that they should go. He made the decision to have each of his children baptized in our youth in hopes that we would accept Jesus Christ as our Lord and Savior. My uncles and aunts too played a role of nurturing us along with their children to believe in God. I thank my God that this act provided the open door, which led me to faith.

Men play an important role in spiritual guidance of the family. God's intent was for man to be good stewards over all he had created and women to help with the process of partnership in this endeavor. Sadly, because mankind sinned against God's original plan, we now suffer the consequent of sin. In most families today, we find a lack of spiritual leadership. I saw this happen throughout our families. The sins of the fathers, as the Bible says, will pass to the next generation. The lack of family unity concerns me and how distant we have all become. The younger people of the current generation seem disinterested in knowing about God.

Despite all the disfunction that passed throughout our family, the good news is, God was merciful and had a plan for each of our lives, and it was because of faith we were able to thrive. His plan for every one of us will never be stopped even when we chose to go our own way. It is my hope that my son and daughter will take the mantle of faith and pass it to their generation.

The Alexanders

Here, you see my parents dressed in their Sunday's best. My mother loved to pose for the camera when she was dressed up. They were committed believers and strived to lead the family with faith as a foundation in our home. My stepfather was our saving grace. He was every bit of the man that my biological father was not. In every way, he was my father, and he will, in my eyes, be the only real father I have known. His support through childhood meant the world to me. He nurtured me through the bullying and the neglect from my mother. He called me his black beauty, and this helped me navigate through the more painful moments. I could run to him and share my feelings, and he would comfort me and assure me it would all be okay. He gave me the confidence to become who I am today. I carry his words in my heart and the memories of the time I had him in my life. He was patient, kind, and he modeled to us what a family man is supposed to be. He walked his talk, and his faith in God was demonstrated in the way he loved our family. He gave of himself as though he was the biological father of all nine of my mother's children, yet he never fathered a child of his own. He was certainly a rare breed. My mother was not the easiest person in the world to get along with, but I truly do not remember him ever raising his voice, or demonstrating anger. If he disagreed with my mom, he would calmly say what he thought and walk away. His love was sacrificial, and he demonstrated a Christlike love. He could have walked away at any time, but I watch him act on the commitment he made to my mother up unto the day she died. My dad passed on November 22 of 2019, and I will always be grateful that God chose him to be my dad. He was still active in Bible studies and participated in feeding the homeless until the Lord called him home. At ninety years of age, he showed me age should not stop you from serving God.

My mother, too, was active in church ministry till her death at the age of eighty-nine. It was not easy to know my mother, and I wished she would have shared her story with me. I didn't understand the struggles, or experiences, that shaped who she was. She, too, had experienced abuse at the hands of my birth father, and mistreatment at the hands of my grandmother. I can only imagine how different it was for her. Some years before her death, I tried to talk to her about our rocky relationship, but she was not open to having that conversation. She made excuses or changed the subject whenever I made attempts to express my feelings. The day before she passed, we all went to the hospital and met with the doctor, who informed us there was nothing more they could do to save her. As she sat, knowing she was going to leave us, I thought this could be the moment she would want to talk to me. Instead, she preoccupied herself in the now-fleeting moments of her life with others in the family and ignored me. She went to her grave not expressing how she felt about me. I told myself to put what I was feeling aside; this was her moment in death, just as it had been in life. Her rejection of me could have affected me the rest of my life had I not been able to recognize it and unassigned her pain to my identity. I had to forgive her inability to emotionally connect and let go of all expectations, or what ifs. I realized even in this there was a lesson to be learned. The lesson for me was finding self-love and self-acceptance. I came to understand my worth through my relationship with God. His Word strengthens me, and now I declare who he says I am. He declares that I am beautifully and wonderfully made. I now embrace my weaknesses and ask God to give me his strength to do better. I have found purpose and a reason for living. I now understand the love of a father that will never leave me, or forsake me. He has gifted me to be a blessing to others, which is the reason he brought me this far. God is in the changing business. He came into my mess to give me a message. He did not leave me the same because I put my faith in him. I believe God sent my stepdad to us for the very purpose of being a spiritual influence in my life. The negative relationship I had with my mother could be why I was so hell-bent on doing things my way. I did not want to look to a God whom I thought would be telling me what I could and could not do. I saw God as a force to stay away from, not run to. I thought God was waiting to judge me for the wrongs I had done. I assumed he would condemn me and send me to hell. Growing up, hell was preached in our churches much more than the message of God's love, mercy, grace, and forgiveness. I later understand, how much God loved me, when he sacrificed his son on the cross to pay for my debt of sin.

I have learned that parenting does not always mean perfection, but provision and direction is the key. They unknowingly—and I say it that way because I never got to share with them the lessons they provided as I was under their leadership—taught me the importance of faith because without it, life could have been more difficult to navigate through, without the joy and hope that God gives. Perseverance was another tool as I watch them go through difficult challenges, making decisions for the family. They demonstrated a level of patience that kept us on course. They showed us what having work ethics was about and the importance of commitment. They gave me insight and the wisdom to be passionate in my pursues for success. I received their spirit of giving and serving, which drives me to be involved in community volunteering. These lessons have been so valuable to my successes and I can only hope I am demonstrating these values for my adult children.

The Gift of Motherhood

God gave me two reason for surrendering my live to Christ. My children, who helped me to stop and see what was most important in life. They were the reason I called on God every day. They gave me a reason to fight against every obstacle that crossed my path. The road was not always easy, but they provided clarity in times of insanity. I wanted to be better because of them. God gave me the responsibility to demonstrate faith for them. I was chosen by God himself to provide an understanding of his love and grace. I took that challenge just as my parents did. I had to stop living in the insanity of repeated poor choices to give them a fighting chance to become responsible, successful adults. Their ability to navigate through society depended on me becoming the example of a parent, who they could trust to drive the ship of our home. God helped me to provide for their financial needs, but there were times I was so busy working, I neglected to see that their emotional need was just as important. I made mistakes no doubt, but after giving my life to Christ, I made faith my priority. Just as my parents pass on faith to us, I too realized my children had a greater chance if they believed God was with them in everything.

I put them in Sunday school and made sure they participated in all children's activities within the church. They had mentors in the church and outside with the big brother and sister's organization. If I could not give them what they needed, I made sure I got others involved in their personal growth.

One Sunday evening I decided to take my children to a church revival. I was so caught up in the service, I did not see my children had left my side. As the minister was calling for people to come forward, I saw my children standing on the stage, professing their faith in Christ publicly. I knew then God's Spirit was drawing them. I was so proud of them taking this step. As they grew older and left home, as many of us do, they strayed, but as I did, they never forgot God was with them and kept prayer and Bible reading in their lives. As adults, they still profess Christ and are on their own spiritual journey. It's important to me that my children hold on to faith in God, but I want them to be active in the next step of Christian maturity. It is important for them to become active in ministry, volunteer work, or some form of community service. Commitment to God is not just giving money and going to church, but it can extend outside the church walls into the community.

Now that my children have refocused their attention toward working out their salvation, I am proud when I have an opportunity to discuss scripture or things they are learning about God. They, too, identify the challenges that come with living in faith, but I am happy I can share my journey with them as it was in the past and what is currently happening in the present. God is involved in the details of their lives like he was with me. We share in that faith together at times, and it means the world to me to know they have not stopped believing. I do worry about my grandchildren and my great-grand-children and the generations to follow. My hope is to pass a message to that generation. God loves you! It might not make sense to you now, but I encourage you to never give up and believe that Jesus died for you. It didn't make sense to me either at first, but having experiences that shaped and develop more faith in my life bought me to writing these words to you. God has a plan for each and every one of your lives. It is my prayer that you will consider asking him to show himself to you. I promise you will not regret it.

I could have never predicted the way my life would turn out. Through the dark times, I could only hope the days ahead would be better. I didn't know how my decision would impact my children, and I could only hope to bring some sense of happiness to their lives. It was not easy to raise them as a single parent, but I can truly say I am proud of them. They are two wonderful people whom I have had the pleasure of meeting, not as just a parent but as friends. This was such a dream in my life to have a different relationship with my children because growing up in my generation our parents were not considered friends, but the authoritarians of the home. The old school methods of raising children was sometimes cold and distant. I did not start off having a close relationship with my children because I used the same parenting style I grew up with. Praise God that I realized it was not too late to correct the dysfunctional way I related to them and as a result the dynamics of our relationship has changed. I celebrate them in all they have accomplished in raising their kids, and I hope to continue cultivating relationships with the next generation. They have made me a proud mother, and I will continue to pour love into their lives and those of their children.

God has given me a new generation of grandchildren and great grandchildren to pass the message of faith to. It is not always easy to have the same influence as I did with my children because I don't have contact with them on a regular basics. Like many families, we live in different cities, and the distance can detroy the bonds that could have been. Talking by phone and video chat is not quite the same as in person contact, yet I do have the constant power of prayer.

People use to use the phase, "A praying grandmother." Well, that's how I fight for the hope that they too will come to know Jesus Christ. I believe in the power of prayer and have seen God do great things in my life through it. I feel the weight of their souls now. I want them to know whatever they go through, God is there, and that he loves them with an everlasting love.

I pray that God will draw each of them by his Spirit to know who he is and the power of his resurrection. I pray as the hardship and heartbreaks of life come upon them they would turn to God and seek his will for their lives. I pray that they understand that this world is not their home as the scriptures teach us, and it is temporay.

Storaging up treasure here will only become trash in the end, but what we do here for God will last through all eternity. I encourage each of you to seek first the kingdom of God and his righteousness, for this is the will of God. Amen!

The Next Generations

The next generation will be faced with new challenges as the world changes. They will have things to contend with that my generation never had to face. I pray they all are able to put their faith in God. I am happy God allowed me to stick around long enough to see my children become parents. I have become a grandparent, and now I am seeing my great-grandchildren coming into the world. I never imagine all these blessings as that young confused woman. There is great joy in knowing my children have put their trust in God and are carrying on the legacy of my faith. I can leave this world knowing God's plan for my life and my children's lives was gifted with his mercy and grace. My heart is comforted by the knowledge that my children have something money can't buy, faith in Jesus Christ.

In addition to my own children, I have brothers and sisters who have passed and left behind my nieces and nephews. I care about their eternal salvation and pray they will come to know Christ. I am grateful to see how some of them are thriving since the passing of their parents. They have successfully managed to start their own families and are now raising their children. I do not know how long I will be around to share with them the hope that lies within me. However, I can pray that the seeds of faith will bring life to them, take root, and flourish in their lives. I love you all, and hope that your journey's will be blessed with God's love, peace, and power.

The Seven Faith Keys

I have told my story with the hopes of inspiriting those I will some-day leave behind. Sharing my life and journey is like giving a thirsty person a drink of water or giving a meal to a hungry stranger. We all have a story, and I encourage anyone reading mine to be sincere and ask yourself some questions about faith. What will you do after reading this story? Will you walk away or ask him to come into your life? I invite you to talk to others and ask if you can hear their story. The Bible too is full of different stories of how God interacted with those before us.

If you need help understanding how to invite Jesus Christ into your life, I have listed seven key points below, which can help you start to build a relationship with Jesus Christ.

Key 1—Ask Him

If you do not know about faith, ask God. If you are uncertain about the claims of Jesus Christ, God said all you have to do is ask. What is a Christian? How do I receive eternal life? How do I know if I really will be saved? You can ask God to reveal himself to you in his word.

> "So, I say to you; Ask and it will be given to you, seek and you will find; knock and it will be opened to you" (Luke 11:9 NIV).

Key 2—Consider Him

Have you ever received Jesus as you Lord and Savior? Salvation is a gift from God. Thank the Lord because he gave his life for your sins on the cross. Eternal life is at stake, do not miss receiving God's free gift. It cost you nothing, but it cost Christ his life as a ransom for your sin.

> "For it is by grace you have been saved, through faith—and this is not from yourselves, it is the gift of God—not by works, so that no one can boast" (Ephesians 2:8–9 NIV).

> "And you, who once were alienated and hostile in mind, doing evil deeds, he has now reconciled us in his body of flesh by his death, in order to present you holy and blameless and above reproach before him" (Colossians 1:21–22 ESV).

Key 3—Confess to Him

God made you, and he decides what is right or wrong. He will be the judge of all the hearts of men. You are responsible for how you will respond to his call to repentance. Admit to yourself and to God that you are a sinner. You might ask what form of sin I am talking about. When we think of sin, we usually think of think of murder, adultery, fornication and more. Do you know just denying Jesus is sin? Yes, there are many more sins we commit against God's holy kingdom, but this is the ultimate act that condemns us to eternal separation from God. When you have ignored God and you wanted to control your own life, you have disobeyed and disregarding God's law. We are all are guilty before him and in need of the savior, Jesus Christ. You must confess and accept Jesus as Lord and Savior.

> "The God who made the world and everything in it is the Lord of heaven and earth does not live

in temples built by human hands. And he is not served by human hands, as if he needed anything. Rather he himself give everyone life and breath and everything else" (Acts 17:24–25 NIV).

"As it is written: None is righteous, no not one, no one understands; no one seeks for God. All have turned aside, together they have become worthless; no one does good, not even one" (Romans 3:10–12 ESV).

"Jesus said, but everyone who denies me here on earth, I will also deny before my Father in heaven" (Matthew 10:33 NKJ).

Key 4—Believe Him

Believe that God loves you and sent his Son into the world to die for you. Jesus took your guilt upon himself and shed his blood for you, and he is the only atonement for our sins. Christ paid the debt of your judgment of sin. This means God has forgiven your sins in the death of Jesus Christ who paid the penalty that God required. God has pardon everyone who accepts that Jesus died for their sin. Putting your faith in Jesus Christ is the only way to restore your relationship with God the Father. Believe that Christ rose from the dead, and he has conquered sin and death. Jesus is alive today and wants to help you live a life that is pleasing to God.

"But God shows his love for us in that while we were sinners, Christ died for us. Since therefore, we have now been justified by his blood, much more shall we be saved by him from the wrath of God" (Romans 5:8–9 ESV).

"Very, truly I tell you, whoever hears my word and believes him who sent me has eternal life and will not be judged, but has crossed over from death to life. He does not come into judgment, but has passed from death to life" (John 5:24 NIV).

"For God so loved the world that he gave his one and only son, that whoever believes in him, shall not parish, but have eternal life" (John 3:16 NIV).

"We were therefore buried with him through baptism into death in order that, just as Christ was raised from the dead through the glory of the father, we too may live a new life" (Romans 6:4 NIV).

Key 6—Receive Him

Have you received Jesus Christ as your and Lord of your life? If you have not taken this step, would you like to pray now? You can pray with someone or alone. Pray what is in your heart and you might want to pray this prayer:

> Father, I have sinned. I have not obeyed your Word. I have tried to run my own life. I have ignored you and your will for me. I have tried to decide for myself what is right and wrong. I deserve your wrath and punishment. I am lost unless you save me. Thank you for sending your Son, the Lord Jesus Christ, to pay for my sin. Thank you for raising him from the dead and giving him authority over my life. I receive Him as my Lord and Savior. I receive your gift of eternal life in Christ. I will turn from my sinful life to serve you. Amen.

Key 7—Walk with Him

After putting your faith in Christ, you must walk with him on a journey of transformation and discipleship. We don't just become good saints overnight. God has given us his Holy Spirit as a guide, and he empowers us to turn from sinful desires. God has called us to take up our cross and follow Jesus. God want us to share our faith with others, just as his disciple did. Many people are suffering in the world without knowing that God is here for them. Your testimony just might save a life from being destroyed from eternal separation from God.

"Then Jesus told his disciples, 'If anyone would come after me, let him deny himself and take up his cross and follow me. For whoever would save his life will lose it, but whoever loses his life for my sake will find it. For what will it profit a man if he gains the whole world and forfeits his soul? Or what shall a man give in return for his soul?'" (Matthew 16:24–26).

Acknowledgment

I am grateful for all the people, places, and situations that brought me to where I am today in my journey of faith. A journey that is continuous and is being orchestrated daily till I see my savior. Like fine tuning an instrument, God's strategically place certain people in place to propel me to each level of understanding. Looking back, I can see how he was so deliberate in every situation, whether good or bad, to work it all together for my good. The good was my spiritual awaking. Becoming a woman of faith was a process that I never saw coming. Here a list of some of the people I am grateful for helping to shape my destiny.

Herman Domino Sr. and Myrtle Tansiel-Alexander, my parents who brought me into the world and gave me the foundation of my faith. Their belief in God was strong enough to influence the direction I eventually turned back to. Mr. Johnson Alexander, who became a true father in the absence of my biological father, his walk in Christ was inspirational to me and gave me hope. He never wavier from his beliefs and demonstrated an example of deep commitment.

Gerald Marcus, my loving husband who encouraged me through every part of the process of writing my story. His support has meant everything to me. He made sure I had the time and energy when needed to continue this project. He was selfless and gave up spending time with me in addition to positive feedback no matter how many times I shared my thoughts.

Tony Spears and Loretta Berryman, my loving children who, without them, much of my journey would not have been shaped the way it was and which brought me to the point of surrendering to

God. They were my motivating force to never get up. Having them gave me a reason to strive and never quit. I want them to know how much I love them and appreciate the wonderful adults they have become. Our talks about faith has meant the world to me. I can see God drawing my children and molding them to carry on the legacy of faith in our family.

Janice King, a dear sister in Christ and a friend who always had my back. God used her wisdom and strong business sense to encourage me to never give up on my dreams to write. I owe her a great deal of gratitude for the times she pushed me and prayed for my endeavors.

Fred Campbell, the senior pastor of Mount Zion Baptist Church was the pastor God chose to develop my understanding of the Gospel of Jesus Christ. The day we met, I promised God I would never walk away from my faith or the church again. I renewed my commitment to Christ under his leadership and was rebaptized in the year of 1985. I was relieved to finally be back in the house of God and reconnected to my roots of faith. Much gratitude to him. There were so many other supportive spiritual sisters and brothers like Richard Echols, Jackie Watkins, Harold and Kathy Lewis, Dave and Caroyln Robinson, Janice Mensha, and so many more.

Through the beginning as a young babe in Christ, I had many strong God-fearing older women who took me under their wings and made sure I understood what faith in Christ meant and how to live it out. The first person I would like to thank is Dorothy Daniels who was my spiritual mother. She made sure I had a foundation of faith, and it was built on a true understanding of God's word. She introduced me to Bible Study Fellowship (BSF), a worldwide organization where you connect with many believers and share the word of God. Then she invited me to prayer meetings where I saw and experience the presence of God's Spirit. Next, her sisters, Cora Harper and Pastor Ida Hardy, who embraced me as family along with the entire group of their children. They were the closest thing to real family since my family was not as close. Over and over, this became the reality of my life in every church I attended.

Lastly, I want to thank Pastor Hurmon Hamilton, senior pastor of New Beginnings Community Church, Redwood City, California. I found humility in this man with a strong message about faith, giving, serving, and the importance of community. He gave me great encouragement that I could achieve writing this book or taking my dreams to the next level. He started life groups within our church, and once again, I was connected to more sisters and brothers. The culture of our life groups, Bible study, and serving in ministry gave my greater meaning. Finding my true purpose throughout the years has been miraculous.

A special thanks to some life group members, Betty Wilson, Bonnie Hill, Zahiya Hasan, Ramonia Villanueva, Kathy and John Vigilizzo, Glen and Vivian Walton, Anthony and Linda Lee, Johnny Cooks, Angelia Birts, and Ruky Tijani, Johanna Torres, Sarah Uyeshima, John and Diana Merida, Darryl and Stephanie Hall, Monica Latimore and Pat Anderson. I am sure I missed some others who too encouraged me to finish this book.

To Angie Ibarra, whom I had the great pleasure of becoming friends and a sister in Christ. You are an amazing woman who have unselfishly given your life to serving under privileged children of Redwood City for nearly a decade. You have been the fruit that remained. I pray God continues to use your life to help many children in the remarkable support for academic learning, food, clothing, but also to see the love of Jesus through all the work you do. I will forever remember our times of serving together and our friendships, which is unbreakable.

I want to say thank you to all the wonderful people God has put in my life, who has made me feel loved and appreciated. Without this village, life would not have been as fulfilling as it has been. Let us, who are followers of Christ, remember to encourage one another. Amen!

About the Author

Dee Domino has a heartfelt desire to have her children, grandchildren, and great-grandchildren understand the importance of having faith. She made a confession of faith at a very early age, but by her teenage years, she had walked away from her beliefs. After facing the consequences of her poor choices, she returned to faith and was able to escape the cycle of drug and alcohol abuse.

Dee successfully went on to higher education, becoming the first in her family to ever attend college, she went on to earn a bachelor's degree in psychology and a master's degree in biblical theology. She was ordained and served in the area of chaplaincy in local jails and prison in addition to being certified to help clients understand the cycle of domestic violence. She felt called by God to use her experiences, as well as her education to help those trapped in addiction and relationship abuse. She saw many lives changed as a result of her obeying God's voice. She continues in ministry as a life group leader and coaches others in these areas for the purpose of empowering and leading others into their journey of healing.

CPSIA information can be obtained
at www.ICGtesting.com
Printed in the USA
FSHW011656240121
77877FS